D0850504

SHORT TALKS
WITH THE DEAD
AND OTHERS

By

HILAIRE BELLOC

Essay Index Reprint Series

BOOKS FOR LIBRARIES PRESS
FREEPORT, NEW YORK

First Published 1926
Reprinted 1967

INTERNATIONAL STANDARD BOOK NUMBER:
0-8369-0192-4

LIBRARY OF CONGRESS CATALOG CARD NUMBER:
67-23175

PRINTED IN THE UNITED STATES OF AMERICA

To

LADY O'CONOR

Contents

Contents (CONTINUED)

Short Talks with the Dead

WHEN I was last among the dead, I had the honour to meet Perkin Warbeck, whom I found at table. He had nearly come to the end of his meal, and was looking keenly through his glass at the light admiring his wine. He seated me very courteously at his side, and I discovered him to be a pleasant spoken young fellow, much more quietly dressed than I thought he would be. I had always taken a great interest in his story, so I made bold, after a little exchange of nothings, to ask him straightforwardly whether he were or were not the heir to England.

He assured me with a light laugh that after so great a length of time he really could not remember.

"Besides which," said he, "if my father were indeed my father (and no man can be sure of that) I am now well out of it all. During my little time on earth I had no inclination for reading, but since then I have passed an ample leisure in the study of history; and, so far as I can make out, the achievement of power is like gold-mining, where a man will spend twenty shillings in washing out a mark. Or again, it is like tight-rope dancing with no interpose of leisure. I am very sure indeed it is not worth the candle."

7

"I agree with you, Sire," said I, but at the word "sire" he waggled his left hand in an affected manner and said:

"A truce to that! Up here (or down here, as some call it) beggars are the equals of kings; though it is true they are expected to keep their distance upon ceremonial occasions."

With that the Pretender bent him again to his *cérises flambées à l'Armagnac* which had just been put before him.

I went on from this trestle board across the asphodel. I had not gone ten yards when a loud shout assured me that George IV, whom I had seen approaching before I left Perkin, had come upon a delicious morsel. But I turned my attention away from these, to regard with curiosity a melancholy but fine-looking gentleman with a pointed beard, who had one of his delicate long hands, his right, upon the golden pommel of a fine staff, the other at his side. A passer-by told me it was Charles I of England, and said to me (noticing my awakened interest) "Would you talk with him? Be sure he will receive you at once. He is most gracious and will talk to the meanest of men as affably as he would to a lord or a money-lender. He owes this virtue to the cutting off of his head which, if I may say so, made another man of him." With that my informant strolled off; for such is the habit among the Elysians—they linger upon nothing for long.

I was eager to approach so great a man, but somewhat abashed. However, his Majesty put me at my ease by extending to me the middle finger of his left hand to kiss, upon which I saw a great diamond as big

8

as my thumb, and cut into a hundred facets. He smiled at me in a melancholy way and said:

"I can see by your eyes that you are yet on earth and I can also tell what your thoughts are. Believe me, I can answer at once what is in your mind. I regret Strafford. I did ill. I am still worried to remember what my wife thought of it. She had an admirable judgment. I consulted her upon every occasion. As for my own death, it was a shock, indeed, and startling, but no such great affair as you make out in your world and much better than the most of deaths. Death for death, better the death by steel than the death of noisomeness."

I told him how abundantly I agreed with him and made bold to say that his death had enriched his country. "Yes, yes," answered he pleasantly, "that is what I always said: I died for the people; for the English people that is. But, alas," and here he sighed, "they have had very little profit by that occasion!"

I was moved to ask him whether he had had an opportunity to judge Oliver at close quarters and under the ample leisure and experience of eternity.

He shrugged his shoulders and answered: "A loud insignificant fellow, borne upward by chance ; very over-bearing."

I answered, "Sir, I think him, from my reading, to have been a hypocrite."

"Of course," answered the King very simply.

"I further think," said I, "that he was slightly mad, as appears in his appetite for cruelty," but the King here became cold and answered me with these words:

"Of that I know nothing: he and I are not of the same world."

9

With that, in order to dismiss me, he extended to me the little finger of his left hand (on which was a fine topaz).

I wandered on through the crowd dispersed in those groves and discovered another passer-by, of whom I asked, "Can you tell me whether the etiquette among you permits me to address yonder proud figure in a wig, who is talking to an obsequious crowd of courtiers—for I make no doubt it is Louis XIV himself?"

My chance acquaintance smiled and answered (having watched my recent exchange with Charles I), "Your head runs on kings! But your error is natural, for this man has got the easy trick of pomposity by long acquaintance. He is not the master, however, but the man. He is not Louis, but the Court Barber; and those who now surround him and bow so low, are the lesser town barbers of Versailles, who very naturally pay him court as the head of their profession."

I was immediately introduced to this talented man, who gave me no time to ask him anything but, on the contrary, questioned me at great length upon our present style of hair and perruque. I told him that in all Europe of to-day, only Actors, rich women, English judges and Clowns, wore wigs, at which he was very much astonished, and even a little perturbed. He asked me how these wigs were made up. I told him that the Clowns' were of a triangular form with three peaks; the Actors' were of all sorts, according as to whether they had to counterfeit bald men of position with greasy curls at their ears, or tousle-headed men of position, or thin-haired men of position, or curly-haired men of position. I also told him that the wigs of rich women were made out of poor women's hair. He then said that he presumed those of the Judges were made up after a fashion to impress the spectator with majesty; but I re-assured him, telling him that they looked more like a horsehair truss than anything else.

The great man next spoke of our faces and begged me to tell him whether the fashion were now for the moustachio, the full beard or the clean Roman shave. I told him that it varied from one country to another; that in France they now affected the silly, silky beard, the Hog Bristle and even the Torpedo; while in England, some of our Labour Party affected the Waxed End and of our poets the Three Days' Scrub ; our bloods, I told him, still wore the Small Toothbrush on the upper lip, and one or two of our wealthiest men the Newgate Fringe.

To all these names of his craft, he listened with an absorbed interest until I added, "Some, very few indeed, have begun to adopt the Whisker." But when I had explained to him what this ornament was, he sprang back as though stung by a serpent and cried:

"I have seen the follies and irregularities of men on a thousand busts and in ten thousand portraits of all ages, but such an iniquity as this I have never seen! What! Small hairy wings clipped to the cheek? Second ears?—and woolly at that? Mocking the true beard and also the Roman austerity? It is intolerable!"

I assured him it was so and that some went so far as to give these badges of shame their ridiculous titles— the Mutton Chop, the Dundreary . . . but he would hear no more, and begged me to leave so disgusting a subject.

11

Turning to the barbers of Versailles, he said severely, "Learn from this, gentlemen, that the human spirit is capable of any extravagance, and that nothing but the discipline of our profession can contain it within due bounds or preserve the decent order of society!"

He bowed to me with the stiff grace of a superior; I left him and approached a melancholy, solitary fellow who wandered along the banks of the stream near at hand, now throwing into it the petals of a flower he held, now strolling half-a-dozen paces with downcast eyes.

"This man whom you are watching," said my new acquaintance, "is a poet, but I cannot discover his name. He is known to us only as ' the poet,' for a jest. He came here young some time ago and has grown no older. It is true that the later comers from your own country talk of him respectfully in his absence, though they give him little honour to his face, but none from the Continent of Europe know so much as his name; and he himself rejects the company of those from the New World, or the Antipodes. He sometimes seeks companionship with his elders, but they do not receive him seriously, saving indeed Theocritus, Virgil, Catullus, and some few others of the very old-fashioned sort.

I approached to address this sad Elysian who looked at me mournfully with very large eyes and asked me whether the second word "forlorn" and "very word" in his *Ode to a Nightingale* did not seem to me out of place and a blot upon the poem. "I sat up two nights," sighed he, "worrying over that line, but I could not mend it. I hate it still."

I told him honestly that, to my shame, I had never read the poem. "No?" he answered, "well, it is not widely known; or, at any rate, was not when I left earth. But I thought you might have happened to come across it and could tell me how it struck a fresh mind. For my part, I cannot bear it."

With that he would talk no more, but turned his eyes again to the stream and clearly desired to be free that he might mutter alone.

Next I saw what seemed to be a very memorable shade. He was a short fat man who paced slowly across the fields with the air of one separate from all his kind; his hands were clasped behind his back, his fine brow oppressed with thought; yet was his face serene and his mouth of an exquisite refinement. A large company moved about him in a sort of attendance. All showed deference, nor dared anyone step beyond his level. He seemed to be in his fiftieth year or thereabouts. I watched his clear features as he pondered and I saw that now and then he smiled charmingly.

As I came up he turned eagerly towards me (for every new face or thing was to him an opportunity for intelligence), and told me promptly and without introduction that he was Napoleon Bonaparte by name and that he could see (for the minds of mortals are within view of the celestials) that I had spent some part of my time in attempting to trisect the plane angle.

"Aye, indeed, Sire," said I.

"Did you solve it?" he asked quickly, "and, by the way, they do not call me ' Sire ' here, nor do I like the title. Have you solved it? Have you solved it?"

13

"Not I, Napoleon," I answered.

As I so replied he pulled a piece of paper from his pocket, on which he had already made certain figures, and, frowning intently, he sat down on the camp stool which a servant spread for him and began with a pencil to make a certain construction (all the while his retinue stood behind him in silence while he worked upon the paper in his hand).

"My God, I've got it!" he shouted suddenly, "and not by any foolery of epicycloids! I've done it straightforwardly, with a construction like the Greeks, simple and final. I've made the Radius Vector EB, pivoting on E, cut the circumference at B, so that its Abscissa AB equals the distance from the point of section A to the centre at O." With that, he proudly put forward to my gaze this construction.

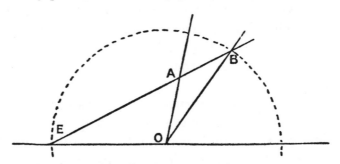

He had done that which for three thousand years men had attempted and failed to do, and I saw pride in his grey, now lifted eyes. But even as I so looked on him the air became full of rumour and noise. The smoke or shadow of a great soldiery filled it, and there came clouds swirling and moving, which seemed like cavalry sweeping by at the charge ; and this

14

mighty armament of ghosts shouted in his praise, cheering the Emperor. He grew larger as I gazed, and the sound about him louder, too. I was conscious of an immense concourse, and of

"The noise of the dead men risen, who warred it in Allemaine,
"When we sprang at the kingdoms with horse hoofs, and we
rang the Republic with songs."

Indeed the clamour became at last so thunderous that I awoke.

Talking of Venice

I READ it in the papers some months ago that they were talking of replacing the gondolas in Venice by motor-boats. I hope they will.

What Venice has lacked hitherto in modernity has been noise. It had crowds of tourists, huge advertisements, bombs dropped on it from the air, newspapers with large pictures of murders, American films and a magnificent publicity : but little noise.

Venice has had whole libraries of books written about people who had written other libraries of books about it. Essays were written on Venice (all exactly the same and quoting Ruskin) by boys and girls in England, Wales, the Six Counties and the Lowlands; by boys and girls of the middle and upper middle classes; 395,288 of those essays were written in 1922 (according to the statistics supplied to me by the present Government) between Thames and Tees alone. Venice already had chemical cooking in a respectable number of restaurants and it had a great many places where you could change money at a loss. It had buildings—palaces and prisons—turned from their old uses into shows. It had all these things. But it had not the essential of modernity which is a deafening metallic noise.

Such noise is the glory of Rome and Paris. I am

glad to say we are reaching a high standard here in London. But Venice is abominably backward in this point. Let them see to it.

While the Venetians are about this vigorous cleansing up of their world and ridding it of the old nonsense, it occurs to me that they might do worse than fill up their canals.

Perhaps it would be too expensive to fill up the Grand Canal, but I am sure the multitude of lesser ones could be turned into reasonable lanes and streets at an expense that would be more than covered by the increased rents of the shops and houses along them. As things are now (or were, when I was last in the town), one had perpetually to cast about for a bridge as one walked abroad, and it made the perambulation of the city exasperatingly difficult. Moreover, the greater part of these bridges are shockingly expensive. They are of stone and even carved. It is a sheer waste and one of which a modern municipality should be ashamed.

Is it not also rather absurd that, to this day, they should keep St. Mark's in use as a church? In Paris, the Sainte Chapelle is no longer encumbered with Masses, Benedictions, Vespers, or whatever they call ceremonies of that kind; it is thrown open to sight-seers at a small entrance fee, and no side-show of little bells, processions or singing or mumbled services is allowed to disturb the intelligent survey of the trippers. That is as it should be. I am told that the new French Government is thinking of doing the same with Notre Dame, and, if they do, all reasonable people will applaud them.

But to return to the filling up of the canals. Every sensible man will agree that the principal use of Venice to modern Italy (which is that of a port), would be increased many fold were the plan of providing the town with proper streets adopted. For, since great ships can only lie in the harbour east of the city, it is impossible for the business and commercial use of the place to expand as long as it is cramped by such ridiculous methods of transport as this smelly labyrinth of narrow ditches. I have statistics to show that a half-mile of progress in Venice in the busier part of the day takes very nearly as long as the journey between the Mansion House and Liverpool Street on a week-day afternoon. What is more ridiculous still— I am astonished how few people appreciate it—is the fact that *there are no wheeled vehicles in Venice.* There are not even omnibuses, let alone cabs!

It used to be said that there were only two capitals in Europe without taxis, Constantinople and Dublin. Since the peace I hear this piece of negligence has been set right by the Turks and the Irish, but it remains true that there are vehicles in every other European town, however backward, saving Venice. To my mind it speaks ill for the dictatorship established in Italy that after more than three years of absolute power, it has been unable to do away with so grave an anomaly in the national life: one at hearing of which every true compatriot of Nathan and Mazzini must hang his head.

There is another very grave indictment against Venice which its citizens will find it difficult to meet. Indeed the verdict against them has already gone by

18

default in all countries of Nordic stock. The water supply is bad.

It is stupefying to remember that even the greatest merchant princes of Venice depended upon water drawn from wells instead of taps, and that no rates were paid even by the wealthiest of them (until quite recent times) for the supply of this very necessary liquid.

The young student of history, particularly if she be possessed of a travelling scholarship or fellowship, might do worse than study the supposed cases of State Poisoning in the old Doges' days and determine what proportion of these unfortunate incidents might be laid at the door of sanitary conditions in those times. It is true that the old Venetian Foreign Office was divided into two departments : the Spying Department and the Poisoning Department. But I am not satisfied that the latter fully accounts for the excessive death rate of the time.

I am the more convinced of this by a discovery that the greater part of this death rate lay in a quite abnormal infant mortality.

I have before me a curve showing the infant mortality among the children of the Doges. It averages at an appalling level, and (what will be more significant to the expert) it is subject to the most fantastic fluctuations; thus, in the case of one Doge (Mariolo) out of a family of twenty-two children none apparently died in infancy, though the average of infant mortality upon the offspring of Doges, in the first complete year after birth, is very nearly 31.03762.

The curve of infant mortality suddenly leaps up to

infinity in the case of the last Doge but three (Tregagni) and all percentage is lost; but it is only fair to admit that in this case there was only one child, and that it perished at the age of 10 months by falling into one of those canals my strictures against which will, I sincerely hope, lead to their abolition.

The bad water supply of the town (which has not really been rectified even yet) has led to another appalling evil, worse, if that be possible, than the dreadful statistics of infant mortality.

The people of Venice, as is apparent to the most casual observer, have been driven by the absence of a proper hydraulic—or perhaps I should say hydrological—system, to drinking quite common red wine habitually as a *beverage*, with all the evils attendant upon so fearful a practice.

I am glad to say that this habit is now somewhat declining among the wealthier classes through the introduction of champagne, Asti, soda water and other common sorts of aerated waters, but it is still appallingly common. Things have gone so far that I have myself observed with my own eyes a priest enter a common bar near the Capo Nero, talk familiarly with the owner thereof, who was his brother, and in broad daylight drink a large glass of red wine as though it were so much milk!

The subject is too unpleasant to be dwelt upon at any length. Nothing but a strong sense of duty has made me touch upon it even in the briefest way.

There are, of course, a number of minor points about Venice which run on the same lines. I have no space to do more than mention them. The town has quite a number of perfectly useless objects, standing about at random, the worst of which is a gigantic tower of brick, set up in the small public square of the city, quite dwarfing it, and ridiculously out of proportion with everything around. This huge blind chimney serves no useful purpose whatsoever. The progressive traveller from the North can hardly credit it when he is told that the monstrous thing was set up of deliberate purpose quite a few years ago to replace an older eyesore of the same sort which had happily crumbled. But the builders of the original tower had at least the excuse of ignorance. They built in the darkness of the Middle Ages. Those who set up its successor were the contemporaries of Mr. Woodrow Wilson and M. Caillaux—let alone Mr. Wallach. They are unpardonable.

By the waterside, close at hand, there still stand two pillars, awkwardly isolated, supporting nothing but a couple of grotesque statues. They remain there simply because no one has the energy to remove them. At certain intervals you will find set up immense wooden poles or masts, unsafe because too thin for their height, painted in garish colours, to the summits of which are attached pieces of cloth; but not even the natives can pretend to explain why these senseless and dangerous toys are permitted.

However, there is some hope for the future. An active group of American and English ladies and gentlemen (with whom are acting, I am glad to say, a certain number from the Dominions) have recently formed a society with offices in Kingsway entitled: "The V.R.C.," or "Venice Reconstruction Company," and there is every hope that when the present irresponsible régime in Italy comes to its natural end, and free institutions are restored, this admirable and disinterested body will be given the concession which it has in vain sought from the existing Government at Rome. If difficulties are still put in their way, they will appeal to the League of Nations.

Talking of Eclipses and What Not

IT is my misfortune that when I write upon what our great modern Lords call "topical subjects" (which means, I suppose—since these Lords are soaked in Greek—subjects on the spot) my very permanent etchings of these are printed long after the matter has ceased to be topical: long after it has ceased to be what Plotinus calls "homocean"— that is, "touching the spot." By the time what I write blazes forth to enrapture the upturned gaze of the myriads, the interest in its matter has wholly disappeared.

So it is now with the Great Eclipse. These most memorable lines are written in the very moment when the sun is fading. They are written just on four o'clock of Saturday, January 24, 1925, being three days after the anniversary of the execution of Louis XVIth, one day before that of the marriage of Anne Boleyn, six days before that of the death of Charles I of England; the day also when Timothy, Bishop and Martyr, ascended the skies.

It is conceded by all that Cricket Matches, Murders and Eclipses are the three chief objects worthy of contemplation by the Soul of Man.

23

To the last I turn; and my first remark upon the Eclipse is this: that it is no small testimony to its place in Creation (if I may use such a term), that upon the morrow of a great Australian Cricket Match, and upon the eve of a great Murder Trial, with both these events filling the minds of those Lords who direct our reading, the Eclipse stands co-equal with the other members of that Trinity.

Were I unanchored in the matter; were I drifting, an isolated soul, uncorrected by the pressure of humanity, I should have thought the thing insignificant.

I notice as I write that it is pretty dark—not so very dark for four o'clock of a January afternoon, and nothing like so dark as it is on an average foggy day at that hour. No one's life is affected; no consequences follow to us upon the matter; no one is the better or the worse. But I bow to the judgment of my kind, and I must admit that the Eclipse is of some strange eminence or it would not thus occupy the chief of our modern English men, and fill the newspapers which they deign to own. I have read that in one great country overseas all the slaves in the manufactories have been set free during the progress of the Eclipse that they may watch the tremendous sight, and I am assured in the same cable that all the millions of that commonwealth are stirred to their depths.

I myself am blind and deaf to such things. There might be an eclipse every day, and I should be none the merrier, nor even the more awe-struck. Sunsets, I confess, move me somewhat, when they are staged with care; and I have delighted in many pretty effects of the dawn. But London, a little less dark, or a little darker, than usual at four o'clock on a winter afternoon leaves me as cold as the hand which Clarimonde laid upon the forehead of I now forget whom—and, indeed, perhaps I never knew.

Nevertheless, I can see how a man driven to it by hunger, or despair, or torture, or the promise of a large bribe, or (what is a more powerful motive) in order to please the beloved, or (what is the most powerful of all) in defence of his own honour, might treat of eclipses in varied, distinct ways, each instructive. For instance, one might make of this Eclipse a pretty text for a dialogue upon Epistemology —as thus:

LEPROS: I perceive, O Thersites, that there is to be, or is now proceeding, or just has been, an Eclipse of the Sun.

THERSITES: You are right, Lepros (by Herakles or Hercules).

LEPROS: Now there are those who say, forsooth, that this strange thing is due to the passage of the Moon indeed over the face of the Greater Luminary.

THERSITES: I am pleased indeed, O Lepros, to hear you use those words, "Greater Luminary." But what of it?

LEPROS: Why then, is it not indeed, upon the one hand, the belief of the vulgar that the Moon is thus occupied?

THERSITES: It is so, indeed, O Lepros.

LEPROS: And what reason have they for that belief?

25

THERSITES: None that I know of. Save, indeed, that they read it in the newspapers of certain Lords.

LEPROS: But do you not yourself believe it?

THERSITES: Why, no, Lepros; by Apollo! I hold with the ancients that it is a dragon eating up the Sun; for the ancients indeed (or forsooth) were nearer the gods.

After this, if one had space (or if anybody could bear such things beyond a very small dose) one might go at length into the reasons which modern men have for believing anything. One might point out in passing that never in the whole history of the world did so many people believe so firmly in so many things, the authority for which they could not test, as do Londoners to-day. It is Print that has done this.

Or again, one might make a very pretty text of the Eclipse on which to embroider a discussion of Design in Nature, after the fashion of the French Deists.

If ever there was evidence of design, it is in the exact fitting of the moon over the sun, like a round shutter cut to size.

For the moon, we are told (I have never measured it) is no larger than a dominion, or Britain Overseas, even smaller than the earth, while the sun is swollen out of all measure; indeed, I have read somewhere that if the sun were an orange (and it sometimes looks like one of a winter evening) the earth would be a grain of shot. And Lord! How little would be you and I? Yet the Sun and Moon are so placed that the moon will give you, now an annular and now a total eclipse of the sun. They almost exactly fit.

26

It is one chance in any number of thousands that they should be placed exactly thus, the moon set precisely at the distance where she does the trick. It cannot be a coincidence.

There is more than this. This Eclipse of 1925 is held on a Saturday, when the Toiling Millions have an opportunity for watching it. What is still more striking, the day is reasonably clear. Now who would not be convinced, under such a convergence of proof, that we here have evidence of Design?

This Eclipse could be used as a text for yet another little sermon: upon the uncertainty of human life. We go our ways, trusting in the normal process of the day; we arrange for the sun to set at a certain hour; for darkness to await its setting; when, oddly, an irregular darkness supervenes: I say deliberately, "supervenes."

Or one might use it for a text the clean contrary way: for a text on the unchanging and awful sequences of Blind Nature in the course of her iron car. It would be a good occasion to bring in the Lucretian tag about the Moon, the Day and the Night, and the stern symbols of the Night. One might cite the dates of past eclipses to prove this, and strike despair into all tender religious souls by a vision of implacable order —crushing us under its wheels.

Or again, one might use this Eclipse the other way about as a text for the annoyance of the historians, showing how very many eclipses noted in the past have come off at the wrong time and were either lied about or broke the rules. Or again, one might use it as a text upon our pitiful ignorance and the vast reserve there is of unknown things.

For an eclipse has all sorts of odd effects, the causes of which are hidden. Indeed, I am told that during an eclipse animals are disturbed and great winds blow. No animal that I could see in London was disturbed, not even a policeman; and it was a dead calm. But no matter.

Or we might use the Eclipse as a Psalm of Hope. The sun is obscured—but it is only for a little time. Soon after it appears in all its glory—or rather it would so appear had it any glory for the moment in January on parallel 51 something North, and near the ocean, and were it not anyhow upon the point of setting into a nasty belt of dull reddish smoke overhanging Wandsworth and the parts about Balham and Tooting.

The more I see of it, the more I discover an indefinitely expanding set of opportunities for discussing the Eclipse, and the more I think of it, the more convinced I am of its complete unimportance.

Yet I am one of those who have taken all the trouble to see a real eclipse, an eclipse in which the sun was put out altogether by the moon, or the dragon, or whatever it is that pulls our leg on these occasions. For in the year 1912 (and I remember it by the loss of the "Titanic") I was determined to see a total eclipse, which in England was not total. I had read that this particular eclipse would be total over a certain band of French territory and that, in particular, one might see it from the Forest of St. Gobain, behind the town of Coucy.

So I journeyed to that place, going the last miles on foot through tall trees, and I watched the darkness fall.

But (if you will believe me) I was moved in that very moment to write a song called "Mrs. Rhys," famous among the wise. And even the air of that great song was suggested to me in that same Forest of St. Gobain as the darkness spread over the world; but the tune of Mrs. Rhys is a sort of mazurka—all of which goes to show that one never can tell. The song was written, the shadow fell, upon that spot where, many years later, the Germans set up one of the Big Berthas with which they shelled Paris, with no effect whatever upon their own doom.

* * * * * *

Whatever more there may be to say upon eclipses, I at least shall not say it. Partly because I have seen no other but these two, both tiresome; partly because I have not the learning to discuss the Theory of Relativity which Einstein stole and which eclipses do so much to confirm, and partly because there is, after all, nothing to say about them. They come and go. That is all. The least smile or frown upon a human face matters more.

Of suggestions conveyed by words (for those who think in words and not in ideas) the Eclipse will furnish a full crop. The Corona will suggest cigars, and at the same time the astonishing facility with which modern men are bewitched by advertisement. The zodiacal light will suggest the zodiac, if you care for *that*; and even if you do not, it will at any rate recall the admirable criticism of Swift upon a contemporary poet who had written that the Zodiac was full of monsters; whereas (Swift pointed out) there is nothing out of Nature in a harmless old man with a watering pot, two innocent twins, fishes, a scorpion, a bull, or a ram; and perhaps only the centaur and the virgin are at all out of the way. The very word "Eclipse" will suggest to you the Derby, racing, and from that a whole world of further maundering.

I freely bequeath all such useful opportunities to my fellow scribblers. I do it with the more generosity and the more pleasure when I consider that it is now too late for them to have any profit of my gift. Unless indeed they save it up for the next Eclipse, and by that time the now ageing and broken men who are compelled to write rubbish at large for a livelihood will (thank God) be dead.

Talking of Byron

ENGLISH people complain that the Continent praises Byron unduly. They say: "These people make out Byron to be a great poet because they are foreigners. They do not understand the full values of the English tongue. Therefore rhetoric, and swing, and ideas appeal to them; but the mystic quality of words, of English words, means nothing to them. They miss that which is the essential of poetry: magic."

Now this judgment I both sympathise with and traverse. I sympathise with the statement that there is no poetry without magic; I sympathise with the natural error that Byron lacked magic, but I call it an error.

As it seems to me, history disproves such a judgment. There is no doubt that his contemporary fellow-Englishmen felt Byron to the full, and that for some reason his fellow-Englishmen of to-day feel him no longer. Or, at least, they do not feel him as they once felt him. If it were true that the foreign appreciation of Byron is essentially a foreign thing, then it would not be true that the England of his day acclaimed him as the chief of poets. But the England of his day did so acclaim him. And the acclamation was not due to a chance fashion, but was personal, profound and sincere. His verse resounded in the English mind by an accord; just as a piece of music will call up intimate enthusiasm, wherein is no hesitation but a complete communion. The appreciation of such verse, all will admit, has been lost to modern England. The modern mania for self-praise would rather choose to say, not that a faculty had been lost, but that greater powers had been acquired; and that the lesser emotions of our fathers had been thrown aside. "The foreigners" (that mania would suggest) "may pick up our leavings. We have outgrown these puerilities."

But wait a moment. What was it in Byron which so moved the men of his time—who were English-speaking and knew nothing but English? That something in his verse *did* move them is abundantly proved. What was it?

In the first place, it was the marriage of *intelligence* with the magic of words.

That there is no poetry without magic all will (I repeat) agree. Magic is the essence of poetry as it is, still more truly, the essence of religion. Magic is that essential which we release when we come to the core of things; and if there be no magic in a religious ritual or a piece of verse, that ritual, that verse, are dead; they have not touched the nerve of reality.

But whereas the magic of religion is actual, the magic of words is symbolic. There is no magic in words which are not understood. The words are symbols, referring the mind to things experienced. Thus if you read the words " . . . and it was dawn upon the sea," the words have no message to one who has not seen, or has not at least some hereditary memory of, that miracle. Even the music of words and the mystical effect of cadence refer to an emotion experienced, apart from the music and the cadence.

Now Byron perpetually strikes that note of experience: the experience of men living as the English of his time mostly lived, and as France, Italy and Spain still mostly live. He struck or recalled or evoked the emotions of men to whom a mechanical industrial life was either unknown or imperfect or irksome. Thus it is the fashion to decry that superb passage upon the sea which begins: "Roll on, thou deep and dark blue ocean, roll," but I will bargain that any man not sophisticated, using the sea, and hearing those lines for the first time, will immediately respond.

The magic in Byron is, then, a consonance with things experienced by men who sailed the sea in ships, not defiling it with engines; by men who saw the landscape of England also then undefiled; by men who slept well, ate well and could drink. It is verse written for men very much alive and normally alive. It is verse written for men who are full of emotion; not jaded, nor needing a spur. Here was a man who expressed what men felt, could not themselves express, but desired to hear expressed. He therefore fulfilled the true function of the poet. For the poet, though divine, is a servant. He is the god in the house of Admetus; and not all his fellowship with heaven would make him what he is did he not bring to birth the struggling song, as yet undelivered in his fellow-men.

Well, this function of expressing, even of expressing

c

sane and normal thoughts for sane and normal days, is apparent in many a chance line of unintelligent writers, struck out by accident undesigned, and flashing an emotion; but Byron united the power to achieve this with the use of the human intellect. That, perhaps, is what our decadence cannot forgive.

We have come commonly to say, in modern England at any rate, that there is between the Intelligence and Vision an incompatible quarrel. This mortal folly (for it is no less) colours all our thought.

You see it in the most important field of all, the fundamental region, that of religion. Men go about talking as though there were between the Vision of transcendental truth and Intelligence, not only a quarrel but an actual contradiction. They are too ignorant to know that the two have been set up together by our ancient masters as the twin and consonant pillars of human life. They are too weak to achieve any such harmony themselves.

You see that modern folly appearing, again, in the preference of humour to wit: for wit is founded upon intelligence but humour upon the neglect of it.

You see it in the muddled worship of what are still called "philosophies"; system succeeding system, and each new system held to be profound in proportion to its incomprehensibility.

You see it in the very mathematic of our day; where mysteries true, but beyond our faculties, are emphasised not because they should make a humble man admit the limitation of the human reason, but because they make small, proud men imagine that the reason is not supreme in its own sphere.

34

All our time is tainted with that contempt of the only faculty whereby man can see and be certain. Yes, even those who think themselves to be rationalists among us are conspicuous by their inability to erect a system of the world, and by their mere piecemeal reaction against the one system which still holds the field—and will for ever: The Faith.

Byron was intelligent and continuously intelligent, and all his verse was rational; nor did he ever subordinate sense to sound, nor common sense to emotion. Now and then, as is the licence of poets, he packs the phrase, and "short-circuits," as it were. But we know very well what he means. When he says of the low brow (the hair of the godlike head coming close above the eyes) that it "might have been desire," that is rather too much shorthand to be rational; but the ellipsis is admissible. At any rate, he never lapses into those two vile weaknesses with which our moderns are paralytically possessed: the itch for mere emotion and the impotence of obscurity.

In this also Byron proves himself a master of verse. For verse is to be conducted like a gunner's team; it is to be controlled like a ship held to a course; it is to be fashioned like a carving out of brute boxwood. It is a conscious creation, though it is aided by a god; and though there is an element of accident in it, yet must that first accident be caught up and continued. The Muse is not a Master but a Mistress (bless her lovely head!). She is to be possessed, not suffered. In a word, the poet is a maker; and in his poetry man the active agent appears as much as he does in his building, or as he did once, when there were statesmen, in the making of policies and laws.

35

To all this Byron adds the supreme quality of continuity. By which I mean that his verse does not flag; that he is strong on the wing; that he maintains a trajectory; that he not only hits his mark, but that all his flight towards that mark is consonant with the end to be attained.

There is not here any question of length. One man does it, as did Milton and Dryden, or as did Byron in *Don Juan*, over hundreds of lines; another in an epigram of two.

It is not a matter of scale but of shape. Wordsworth, I will steadily maintain, never wrote even a sonnet, let alone a longer piece, in which there are not the most damnable breakdowns—like an athlete sitting on the floor exhausted in the midst of his performance. And I take Wordsworth as the obvious antithesis to Byron. But it is also true of all those whom men contrast with Byron. Thus it is true of Shelley. When Shelley wrote: "I arise from dreams of thee," he wrote something with more lift in it, perhaps, than Byron ever managed, and certainly with more subtlety of rhythm. But the long efforts of Shelley are full of balderdash. The man with a sense of continuity —which is Form—stops when he cannot go on. He leaves out what is below the level of his flight or, rather (to be more accurate), he is gifted with a sense of his frame and works to a mark.

Make you, also, no error on this: the time in which we live is a time of confusion, not untouched by despair, very wearied and awaiting change. Byron will survive our time and will stand among the very great poets of England. Our misapprehension of

36

him is due to *our* change, not Poetry's; and our change has been for the worse. But we shall recover, and his star will reappear with the dissipation of these nasty mists.

Talking of Livy

NOT so long ago a jolly fellow said he had found the lost books of Livy.

Had the lost books of Livy (Decades, I am told, I should call them) turned up after all, it would have been great fun, for there would have been a re-writing of Roman history and from the infallible pedants one of those amusing confessions of fallibility to which we have now grown accustomed every few years. They come at regular intervals. They disguise themselves usually, do these confessions of error, under the mask of an expanded knowledge, but they are not that. They are avowals of mistakes, exposed by further discovery and no longer to be concealed. The long series of them has now, to the great delight of all honest men, thoroughly shaken false authority.

But though it would have been delightful to have watched the upset from that secure shore of ignorance and common sense whence we lesser mortals watch the academies tossed on the troubled sea of charlatanism, yet there are other things arising in my mind in connection with that affair.

The first thing that so arises in my mind, my ignorant mind, is the soft, suffused air of delight evoked by the word "Livy." It is one of the very few left of those idiomatic English names, transformed from the Latin, which we can still boast.

Our fathers used to call Cicero "Tully," and we still talk of Ovid and of Virgil and of Horace. But for the most part the Latin names have broken back upon our tradition and have re-established themselves. It is an evil and the symptom of an evil; for an idiomatic form given to classical names betrays a familiar and intimate knowledge with the work for which they stand: makes them part of the furniture of an English house. I could wish that Catullus were "Catull." Martial and Juvenal, by the way, still stand—I had forgotten them; but I could wish that we had for Julius something corresponding to what the French have made of the word when they say "Jules," and that we had "August" for Augustus, as we do still have Trajan and Hadrian and Constantine and Gregory. The native terms seem to have taken root under the influence of religion.

It seems as though the names with which the Middle Ages were most familiar were allowed to put on a proper English dress: Bennet, Austin, Hilary, Jerome, Cyril—but not "Method."

But there is more than that about "Tite-Live," as they call him over the water. There is the virile simplicity, the straightforwardness of his pen: very different from his successor, Tacit. There is the jolly jingoism of the fellow in which any honest man must, should and shall revel.

I had a long discussion some seven years ago, lasting far into the night, with the headmaster of one of the great public schools. The discussion turned upon a subject on which I was put down for a debate at the Cambridge Union that autumn—I forget for the moment whether for or against—to wit, "Whether the teaching of false history be not necessary to the State." Livy had no doubts. He was for the legend, first, last and all the time. He felt it in his bones that the greatness of Rome was to be supported by as much pro-Roman legend as he could manage—and he never faltered. He had the religion of patriotism—and I have known worse :

"*Et si cui populo licere oportet consecrare origines suas et ad Deos referre Auctores, ea belli gloria est populo Romano ut cum suum conditorisque sui parentem Martem potissimum ferat tam et hoc gentes humanæ patiantur aequo animo quam imperium patiuntur.*"

There is something else about Livy (indeed, the subject is inexhaustible, like all subjects except Unity; and I am not sure that one could not make a shelfful of books about Unity if one were driven to it): he is a writer of prose.

I do maintain that in prose-writing it is a very great virtue indeed to write prose and not to confuse it with rhetoric or verse. Not that I have a word to say against rhetoric: it is a very nice kind of permanent and sustaining music, but it is not prose; and verse is a condensed, distilled sort of thing (at least, good verse is) which the prose writer, while he is writing prose, will do well to put entirely out of his mind. Livy did not, and could not, have written the "*Tantæ molis erat Romanam condere gentem,*" but his prose was inspired by the idea distilled into those six words. And he expressed it as a prose writer should express every-thing, that is, with the purpose of getting his whole thought and its colour transported undimmed into another mind: lucidity.

Yet again, Livy is the father of those (good luck to them!) who write, and write, and write, and write, and write, and write, and write—and then go on writing. Whether he was compelled to do so or simply did it from wantonness, I know not; but, at any rate, he did it, and in this way may be regarded as the ancestor of those Fathers of the Church who produced so gigantic a volume of volumes that one would think they did nothing but dictate—which was, indeed, the case. Yes, even in their sleep.

Surely also Livy must have dictated. Had it be-come the fashion by his time? I don't know. At any rate, if he was not too prolix in style (and some say he was; God knows: I do not), he was exceedingly productive of thousands of words. I hope he got his price. This man Livy (I am beginning to grow enthusiastic) shovelled out work by the ton, and another literary fellow living a little after his time complained that his library was not large enough to house the total Livy. Take heart, therefore, you my fellow hacks, and when men jeer at you for writing and still writing, answer over your right shoulder: " Livy," and turn to the task again.

Nor does this exhaust my beloved Livy. He is one of those writers whom every man can honestly say that he has read. Yes, I who am writing this, and who have little Latin and less Greek, can honestly say that I have read some pages of Livy. Men commonly lie when they pretend to a knowledge of Dion or of Bion or of any other Lion, and they lie abominably when they cite Justin Martyr and St. Augustine; and they lie impudently when they pretend (but who of our generation still dares so pretend?) to have read that great pillar of Europe, St. Hilary of Poitiers, upon the Trinity. They lie as a rule when they pretend to Hesiod. They often lie when they pretend to Theocritus, and they lie disgustingly when they affect a familiarity with Plautus, because they happen to remember one tag. But every man can stand upon his two feet, square to the world, and say: "I have read some pages of Livy." And in this that historian stands side by side with a great twin ghost, another Gaul of Lombardy as Livy was, a man whose name leaps at once to your lips as to Catullus' grateful mind, Cornelius Nepos. I am not sure that Julius Cæsar is not jealous of Livy, and that they do not bicker when they meet in those quiet fields which I also desire to attain, beyond the rivers of forgetfulness and of death. For even though Julius Cæsar's commentaries upon the Gallic War were written (as it has pleased a German to say—but we are getting tired of Germans) by his tutor (and if they were, I hope the tutor soaked him well and came in handsomely on the list of creditors), yet Cæsar, I am sure, does in the Champs Elysées preen himself on authorship and thinks of Livy as our highbrows think of our best-sellers; to which Livy can answer by jingling a few coins in his pocket and passing on easily with a smile.

What else of Livy? He is dead. That is not much

to say of any man. His fame has survived, or at any rate his name has, and that is a great deal to say of any man. Of his vices we know nothing. Of his virtues less. It is his *œuvre* which has survived and which clothes Livy. Oh, fortunate in this! Oh, three times and four times blessed! That what he wrote is his sufficient monument, and that the sensitive human instrument in him escaped publicity! I can call to mind no Don who has written a life of Livy, though Taine did write a treatise. He is not stuff for problems, and he kept somewhat apart from the smart women of his time, and from the sham austerity of their counterpart, the Court of Augustus.

And what else of Livy? Why, to conclude with: Livy having set it down in his histories that such and such things were certainly done, has, of course, been the butt of all our new criticism. He said that the French came over into Italy from the N.W., which is where you would expect them to come from. They still come over from that direction to-day. "The Turinian Passes and the Doria"—for who (in the face of all the surroundings, the Ticino fighting, the proceeding *onwards* to the site of Milan) would accept the "Juliæ" reading? Eh? Thou XIXth century doubter? Thou Boche? Thou Prehistoric Ass? But our moderns are careful to explain that the French did nothing of the sort, but came over from the Germanies and by the Brenner and to the east thereof. In this, therefore, Livy is our brother, for he also is subject to being set right by dwarfs and to suffering the fantasies of fools.

I hope, then, that when I meet my Livy on the far

43

side of the Ferry, this suffering at the hands of fools may be a sufficient bond between us, and that he will introduce me to that club, of which Lucian is the secretary, and election to which is my very dearest desire.

The Good Poet and the Bad Poet

ONCE there was a poet who wrote such beautiful poetry that he became immensely rich and built a large house of red brick in Fitzjohn's Avenue, Hampstead; where he lived surrounded by his friends, the Good Architect, the Good Painter and a few others of the same sort who had, like himself, made gigantic fortunes by their excellence in their respective arts.

One night about Christmas time, this Good Poet was coming home in his Rolls-Royce from dining with the Lord Mayor of London. It was nearly midnight, there was no moon and there had been a deep fall of snow. Just as the motor was turning into the gate of his Splendid Mansion, he felt the wheels bump over something and was much annoyed to conjecture that a log must have been left lying in the fairway, but the Second Chauffeur (for he always had two men to drive him) jumped down and told him in respectful tones that they had had to pull up because they had run over a man.

The Good Poet's first impulse was to bid them drive on and disregard the obstacle, but his better nature

45

and a fear of paragraphs prompted him to give orders that the fellow should be picked up and taken into the house.

Luckily for him who had thus impertinently lain in the gateway of the Good Poet, the snow had already covered him so deeply that he was not very badly hurt. He had fallen inanimate from lack of food some hours before, and his chief danger seemed to be the catching of a chill from his exposed position. When they had thawed him in front of the great kitchen fire, and given him a basin of skilly, some stale bread crusts and a glass of pure cold water from the tap, he revived sufficiently to murmur a few words; and the Good Poet, having heard the state of affairs from his Groom of the Chambers (to whom the Butler had made report upon the evidence of the First Footman), was so charitable as to order that the fellow should be allowed to lie all night in the garage, with a few rugs to keep him from freezing to death; he even added that he might be given some sort of breakfast the next morning. Further, he was not to go away until the Good Poet had seen him, in order that he might make sure that there should be no trouble about Third Party Claims. For it had been the unfortunate experience of the Good Poet (as of all wealthy men, alas!) that even the humblest of the poor may be driven to some dirty act of ingratitude at the solicitation of a base lawyer who shares the swag.

It so happened that next day the Good Poet gave one of his accustomed great luncheon parties, at which were present all manner of famous men: Generals and Politicians, Judges, Men who Promoted

46

Companies, Owners of Newspapers which printed news of murders and other exciting things and put in pictures of people under sentence of death, famous Divines and even Bankers. Indeed, not a few of the Guests were Peers.

The luncheon was over, and they had all retired to the Good Poet's library, where they were drinking bitter coffee with Armagnac, Cointreau, Grand Marnier, Arquebuse, Izzarra of the Basques, Strega, Calvados, and other commoner liqueurs such as Brandy, Kümmel, Curaçao, Benedictine and Crême de Menthe itself, when the Good Poet, whose brain was always more active under the influence of conversation and its accompaniments, suddenly remembered the poor fellow who was still thawing down below. He therefore desired a Bishop among his Guests to touch the electric bell at his side and, when a liveried servant had answered the summons, he asked for a report upon the stranger. The Domestic bowed low and returned in a brief time with the account that the man was now fairly restored, his clothes were nearly dry and he had been given some more skilly and bread for his mid-day meal.

"You must know," said the Good Poet, "that this unfortunate man had fallen from exhaustion before my gate, and I thought it only decent to have him taken in and looked after." At which the assembled Guests murmured their appreciation of so much goodness, and the Bishop said, "For my part, I thank you personally from my heart for your Christian Deed."

"Let us have him brought up here," said the Good

47

Poet, "it is quite possible he may have something interesting to tell us; for these tramps often have odd adventures."

The man was therefore brought up and came in among all these great people very shamefacedly and awkwardly. And, indeed, it was a difficult moment, because his clothes were hardly decent and had obviously been ready-made, even when they were new; while his boots were burst and presented a very disgusting appearance.

But the Good Poet, who was a Man of the World, affected not to notice all this, and asked the stranger (who stood before them nervously twiddling an offensive and greasy cap) who he might be.

"Sir," said he, in a low, despairing and feeble voice, interrupted by a dreadful cough, "I am a Poet. Alas, my dear mother often warned me to take to some more solid profession, but I was young and would not heed, and now she lies in the quiet churchyard of ——"

"Yes! Yes! We will take all that as read," said the Good Poet who could not bear *longueurs*. "But surely you must have been singularly bad at your trade to have reached the position in which we now find you?"

The unfortunate man (whom we will now call the Bad Poet) hung his head and suffered severely the indignant and reproachful glances of the seated company.

"It may be so," he admitted unhappily, "no man is a judge of his own work; and certainly I have had no fame, nor have I even been able to sell my verses, so I suppose they cannot be good, any of them; and yet I have been proud enough of some, even when they

48

were sent back to me by American and other editors. And though I may not have done anything really good yet, perhaps, if I keep plodding away, I shall be able to achieve something of value before I die. But the trouble is that I get exceedingly weak from lack of food and from the inclemency of our climate, especially in the winter months."

The Good Poet, who knew from long experience the signs of mendicancy, stopped him short at this point and changed the direction which his talk was taking.

"Suppose you recite us some of your stuff. Have you anything that you retain in mind?"

"Yes, sir"—("Charles," interrupted the Good Poet, "Sir Charles, if you please"). "—Yes, Sir Charles, I am even now composing an Heroic Poem upon Wine. I have been at it four years, but alas, it is not yet completed, for I fear I am a very slow composer."

"Never mind that," said the Good Poet, "let's have it, or bits of it at any rate." And they all settled back in their chairs, while the Bad Poet, after a terrible fit of coughing and leaning with one hand upon an inlaid table, because he felt very weak after standing so long, began as follows:—

To praise, revere, establish and defend;
To welcome home mankind's mysterious friend;
Wine, true begetter of all arts that be:
Wine, privilege of the completely free;
Wine, the foundation, wine the sagely strong;
Wine, bright avenger of sly-dealing wrong—
Awake! Ausonian Muse and sing the vineyard song!
Sing how the Charioteer from Asia came
And on his front the little dancing flame
Which marked the godhead. Sing the panther team
The cymbal and the thrysus and the gleam
Of bronze among the torches. . . .

D

"Come! come! come!" said the Good Poet, "we can't go on like this for ever!" To which all his Guests nodded assent. "Give us a patch out of the middle, but spare us."

The Bad Poet, after yet another fit of coughing, hesitated for a word and began:—

> . . . . . Where
> Upturned to Heaven, the large Hipponian Plain
> Extends luxuriant and invites the main;
> Or where, festooned about the tall elm-trees,
> Etrurian grapes regard Tyrrhenian seas;
> The . . . .

"This will never do," said the Good Poet impatiently. "Give us the very end and let's have done with it."

The Bad Poet, his voice now failing from exhaustion, looked plaintively at them a moment and then murmured:

> When from the void of such waste labours done
> I too must leave the grape-ennobling sun,
> Turn to the home-lit plain my grateful sight
> And leave the mountain to the advancing night;
> When the poor end of such attempt is near,
> Just and benignant let my youth appear,
> Bearing a chalice, shallow, golden, wide,
> With benediction graven on its side.
> So touch my dying lip, so bridge that deep,
> So pledge my waking from the gift of sleep
> And sacramental raise me the Divine:
> Strong Brother in God and last Companion: Wine.

"Is that the end?" said the Good Poet. "Yes," whispered the reciter, miserably, and then again began to cough in a really exasperating manner.

"It is very bad," said the Good Poet, "very bad indeed. Now if you want to know why you have failed and the difference between your stuff and the kind of thing I write, listen to this, for I also have written a poem on Wine—it is much shorter than yours and much better."

With that he lifted himself out of his easy chair, all his Guests rising at the same time, out of respect. He took from a shelf a magnificently bound book which was very thin, and, indeed, consisted of only four pages, on one of which only was there any printed matter. This the Good Poet opened and read:

"Wine exercises a peculiar charm.
But, taken in excess, does grievous harm."

He then reverently kissed the page and replaced the volume, while his guests broke into a buzz of applause.

After that supreme experience, there was nothing more to be done.

The Bad Poet was dismissed—and it only shows how true it is that good deeds bring misfortune in their train, that the Bad Poet died on his way downstairs, giving infinite trouble to his benefactor, whose party was spoilt by the wretched accident and who had to send for the Poorhouse Authorities to get the corpse out of the way.

The moral of this is, if you can't write good verse, don't write any at all.

Talking of Fakes

I HAVE never understood why a good fake should not be as valuable as an original. If a man can reproduce an article so that not one man in ten thousand can tell the difference between the model and the copy, what element is it in the model which gives it its value? I can understand its having a special value, if it is an object of peculiar historical interest. For instance, the actual sword which Cromwell wore at Naseby would be amusing, and one would be annoyed to find that one had been palmed off with a copy. But when it comes to reproducing a Chippendale chair, or an old frame, what does it matter whether you have the form as it was first put forth, or its exact double?

This lack of value in reproductions handicaps one of the very finest efforts of mankind. For me, at least, there is nothing more marvellous than the making of fake bindings, fake furniture, fake armour.

I had an expert once show me in a great hall in Sussex exactly how he could tell a piece of fake armour from an original. I have forgotten how he did it; but I know there was something about the structure of the metal on looking at it through a magnifying glass. But if my pleasure in looking at armour is a pleasure in its decoration and shape, what should it matter to me whether I am looking at a thing new or old?

I think we owe great gratitude to the hosts of men who have learned how to make counterfeits. Their art has all sorts of qualities over and above the quality of creation. They bring to bear upon a useful illusion a mass of talent which we could never set to work in any other connection, and which is really so prodigious in amount and kind that I perpetually marvel at it. I have known a man who could make you a duplicate of a water-colour drawing so exact that a man who had lived with the original all his life could not tell the two apart.

You might take him an 1840 picture of the Grange, Little Biddleton, where dear Grandmama died. He would bring you back that same picture of the Grange, Little Biddleton (where dear Grandmama died), so that you received it with tears of reminiscence. There was the foxed mounting, the plain, rather dull and simple gilt moulding, with a chip off it here and there showing dirty white, and even the little gape at one of the mitred corners. There was the old stucco house, rather out of drawing, the absurd trees, and the abominable pale green lawn. It was the thing you had seen on the landing all your life; the thing Aunt Betty had painted. But no. It was a copy. And when you had gazed upon it long enough, and asked to see the copy, the original was produced.

I have talked to some of these great men, but they are careful, and I never learnt more than a very few tricks of their trade. One of them did tell me of the way in which the minute worm holes are made in

53

imitation of old wood. They are made by shooting at it with fine shot from a certain distance. That's how you get the haphazard distribution. Another man told me how you made the old card tables go. When you had rubbed the green cloth enough, and spilt a little ink on it and cleaned it off again, and broken a tiny bit out of the inlay, and so forth, the next thing was to make it wobble a little. You cut off the merest trifle from one of the four feet, and in that way it wobbled and was old. Then the purchaser would come along, and if he did not notice the broken little bit of inlay or the wobble, it was up to the seller and maker to point both those things out to him, and to say that was why he sold it so cheap, and why he was prepared to let it go for seven hundred and fifty pounds. Moreover, if his client desired it, he was game to repair the inlay, and to put a shred of wood on the offending leg, and charge nothing.

Now all this is good; it is good for the buyer who has his will (+ the defects mended); it is good for the seller—£750 is very good; it is good for the world which has two old looking tables in good taste, instead of one. No one loses, everybody gains.

The people who fake things do good to mankind in yet another manner. They expose the absurdity of labels. There was one man for whom I had a very great admiration, who faked some Wordsworth sonnets, thirty years ago or so in the London Press. If I am not mistaken, the first paper he took in was one called the *Pall Mall Gazette ;* but all the rest followed like sheep. He said he had got them from an old shepherd in the Lake Country. He lied. They were very bad sonnets. One of them, I remember, ended up with the words, "Man liveth not by bread alone," and had something to do with the Corn Laws. They were just the sort of sonnets Wordsworth would have written. So they were as perfect in the fake line as they were imperfect in the poetry line. He waited until he had thoroughly and wholesomely duped the Pantheists, and collected all their praises; then, and only then, did he tell them how he had pulled their leg.

And this reminds me, that, related to the great fake department of art, is its counter-part, which passes off famous originals as obscure and worthless.

Thus it was the diversion of gay rogues in my youth to take some few lines out of the longer poems of Keats, and not only send them to a highbrow editor, but add that the writer valued his opinion far more even than acceptance of his verse. These verses of Keats always came back, and usually with such a kind letter from the editor! He would write and tell us exactly what he thought about them, and how they betrayed the faults of youth, and where the promise in them lay. It was great fun.

Another man, I remember, worked it admirably upon the Customs, the American Customs, in a matter of painting. He had bought, let us say, a Corot, signed. He would approach a person well trained in the Faker's art, and get them to paint over the Corot signature another commonplace signature, such as Perkins. When that had well dried, a Corot signature was again painted over on the top of the Perkins. So far so good. Before the picture came to the New York Customs this honest dealer would have started a correspondence in the Press, saying that a supposed Corot which was awaited for such and such a collection (his own) was a fake. A man of straw, put up to protest the Corot,would demand of the Customs people that the signature should be scraped. He would firmly promise to guarantee the damage. The top Corot signature would be scraped off, and Perkins appear underneath it: the value became negligible, and the duty with it. Then, all at leisure, when the thing was forgotten, Perkins in its turn was scraped off, and the real Corot signature reappeared.

The truth is that the psychology, the absurd psychology, of the purchaser of originals, has never been dealt with as it should be, save in one case, which I know of, and which was that of a French Court of Justice.

There was a Frenchman who found in an old house on the Loire an admirable Francis I chair. He could get no fellow to it. He took it to a fake furniture man in Paris, and gave the order for another eleven exactly similar to be made, so that he might have a dining-room set of twelve. When the eleven came, they were quite unlike the original. All sorts of little details were wrong. The man refused to pay, and the thing was taken into Court. The decision of the Court was that the furniture maker should make a twelfth chair exactly like the other bad eleven.

Which reminds me. One of the best pastimes in the world is to take a man who boasts of the Middle Ages, and of his tender sympathies therein, to the Door of Notre Dame in Paris. Show him how carefully the

Last Judgment has been restored after the XVIIIth Century Dean and Chapter had cut through it, and how you can hardly tell the old from the new. Then ask him whether he can pick out which of the big statues of the Apostles below are XIIIth Century and which are Viollet le Duc. He will make a careful selection; and when he has done that you have the pleasure of telling him that they are all new.

The Opportunity

THREE men had met in a vacant college sitting-room at Oxford after a gaudy. The sitting-room was assigned to one of them who was sleeping in college, the other two had rooms in a hotel in the town, and all were to go up to London together the next morning. They were nearly contemporaries; round about fifty. Not one of them overlapped the next by more than a year, and the eldest knew the youngest fairly well. The eldest was a squire of the country between the Wye and the Severn, wealthy, hating publicity; keen on two things, Arabic and fishing. The second was a lawyer who had made for himself a very great newspaper name indeed and was shallow and ill-bred, but also bitter; a little mollified that night by his return to places of his youth, and those who had been his companions. The third it would be difficult to describe. He might be called a traveller—though that is no profession. He was an only son. His father had left him money under trustees, the income of which fluctuated between £1,800 and £2,000 a year before the war. He was a bachelor. He had spent his income when it was sufficient (and even now, after the war, when it had become insufficient), in wandering about. He added to it by occasional articles and an occasional book, very well written (though he had not himself the least idea what people meant when they praised his style). He made no attempt to add to that income in any other way; and now that money was so much less valuable than it had been, he travelled as far afield as before, only much less comfortably, preferring novelty to ease. Luckily for him, he had no expensive taste.

Of these three, the squire was a large lumpish man, rather bald. What little hair he had left was grey and curly on either side of his head. He spoke slowly and with the hesitation of the scholar. The lawyer was voluble and had upon his face, which was otherwise strong, though shifty, the marks of many years of excess. The traveller was tall and lean with one of those hatchet faces which promise more energy than they really possess. He had very piercing eyes, a firm, thin mouth, and believed, so far as England was concerned, everything he read in print; for he had not been born quite into the rank of the gentry and he had not got his foothold firm; nor did he want to get it so. On the countries he had visited, other than England, he trusted his own experience.

Each of these men, being a man, had a worm at his heart, eating it out.

The squire had this worm at his heart. He was well married with fine, healthy children; the son married in his turn and well married; of three daughters one also well married, the other two, young, happy and advancing into womanhood. He was in no way encumbered, in no way harassed by any external thing. But he had once desired with a passionate desire, and

59

through his own lack of courage he had failed to seize opportunity.

The woman still lived; he still met her often enough. His soul was, as it were, doubled. One deadened, despairing part of it, lived on year after year amid realities; the other lived by itself in visions. For though he had missed his opportunity, and though he certainly desired after a fashion in which he was not himself at all desired, yet that hidden influence which alone can build a bridge between two souls, *had* built such a bridge; therefore his failure to seize his opportunity all those years ago now rightly tortured him, and therefore he had some substance to go upon in his false world of imaginings, compared with which his world of realities was a despair.

The worm at the lawyer's heart was of a meaner kind, but very sharp in the tooth. He had always had for his goal, from the first day when he had begun to make a noise in the University as a boy, a sort of vulgar triumph: an easy priority. He had imagined that his life would continue to be a life of that kind; but life (and the Commons) undeceived him. He had had to eat dirt steadily from his twenty-fifth year. He did not know, when he began, how heavy was the price of publicity. He had desired it and he had purchased it piecemeal; but at every step with humiliation, with the swallowing of insult; with the restraint of vengeance; under the sneer of those who were at one moment or another always his masters, and under such a sense of dependence (now that he was at the very summit) as bent him down, like twenty pounds of lead swung round his neck.

60

There is only one way out of that prison (voluntarily entered but, once entered, not to be evaded) and that way is debauch. He had very freely used such a key. Therefore to the despair of the soul were added increasing fits of physical depression, which are the wages of debauch.

He also had had his opportunity—how it haunted him! Very early—before his thirtieth year—when he had accumulated but a few thousand pounds, he might (by an investment which an odd chance put before him) have turned his savings into a very large fortune indeed, and that quickly. He would never have had to climb, he would never have had to lick other men's boots or to swallow insult, or to suffer any of his wounds along that painful way; he might even have kicked the House of Commons from under his feet and become a free and honourable man. For mark you, adventurers of this sort have in them always a lingering appetite for freedom and for the honour they have lost. But he to whom calculation, intrigue and the nasty analysis of men's weaknesses had been a special combined talent, lost his opportunity through miscalculation, through a misunderstanding of men. He had made a sideslip in financial intrigue. He still earned a very large income; but to this day he was still hopelessly in debt.

The case of the third man, the traveller, was simpler. The worm at his heart was the loss of a religious vision. To put it plainly, he had once seen, not paradise, but the light that shines from paradise, and had been called to a certain effort, to witness to the Faith : the reward of which would have been—*at last*—secure beatitude. To him, a man inspired by great hill ranges, and with his mind full of landfalls caught suddenly from far out at sea, beatitude was naturaı and a need. He had had his opportunity. He had lost it; not through lack of courage, heavy as are the penalties of Truth, but through sloth. An effort had been required of him in that decisive moment long ago: a certain tearing apart of habits; a virile decision; a firm grasping of the helm and a twist of it. But he had postponed, lingered, waited—and the opportunity was gone.

These three men sat over the fire of an English July evening, in the small hideous college sitting-room which owed its architecture to Ruskin, with the few books of some unknown undergraduate in the deal sheives upon the walls, with one or two photographs and one or two prints, very deplorable. With what was much better, a large tobacco jar of wrinkly brown having upon it the college arms in monstrous colours, and what was better than all of these, with a worn photograph upon the mantelpiece of a reasonably good woman.

They did not exchange commonplaces : men who have been boys together never do that. They were wary each of the others; yet their talk drifted to the chances of life and each said as they discussed the oddity of fortune (each patronising the others as he did so) that if they had their lives to live over again, they would live them much as they had lived them, but perhaps make something of a better job of it. Each in his heart wished that the talk had taken another turn and hungered passionately for the opportunity each had missed.

62

Just as they were about to break up, and (the two of them who slept out) to say good-night, a young man came in, tall, handsome, dark, brisk, unpleasant. He stepped back a moment, as though he had thought the room empty, then apologised, went quickly to the shelf of books and took a book therefrom; then, as he went out (they having already risen to break up), looked at them with eyes too summoning and said with a smile which haunted them, this extraordinary thing, "Ye're all of ye wanting your youth, is it? Ye'll have it!"

He shut the door noisily behind him; they grinned at each other conventionally, and the lawyer reminded them how there was a madman of that sort among the undergraduates of their own time. For in their own time there had been a famous lunatic who thus used to pretend to probe suddenly into the lives of men quite unknown to him, and who had had the insolence to try the trick on his seniors.

The next morning these three men forgathered upon the platform of the station and got into the same railway carriage together. There was no one with them and no stop before Paddington. They had already talked on the platform about their mad visitor. As they sat down for the journey each took up his paper to see the news, each remembered what had been in his heart the night before: in each the lost opportunity of youth had been stabbed into life by that insane ejaculation.

The first to put down his paper and look up from it was the lawyer, the second was the traveller. They were both Englishmen and both men of control, yet

63

each gave a suppressed cry, for each had become young, the faces were the faces each had known nearly thirty years before. When the squire put down his paper in his turn he was more perturbed, for he was less experienced, and he caught the air for a moment with his hands as though he felt a sort of dizziness. He saw their faces and they saw his, the easy, the eager, the ready untouched faces of those distant years.

Now such is the action of men in society, of men long mixed with other men and long corrupt, that no one of these three betrayed what each believed to be a passing illusion. But as their conversation continued, each grew convinced that indeed the miracle had taken place; that something had interrupted the iron sequence of time, and that opportunity had been restored. Each in his heart went through a violent revolution, looking forward now and no longer backward. Each had the eyes of the soul fixed intently upon the Opportunity which now would come again. It would come! The second chance would come! Each was in a mood so exalted that the immediate results of such prodigious things did not affect him; each felt a confidence that not only their own time, but all time had rolled backward. In each there was a growing certitude that the years between had been imagined as a sort of warning; that their lives had been dreamt lives, and that they themselves and all England were still young: that it was still 1897.

But the lawyer, more accustomed to proof, put a test to himself. The woods were the same and the river; but they would pass a station that he knew (he might have looked at the date on the newspapers and

64

verified their contents, but even his strict mind was bewildered).

He said to himself, "I shall recognise the old station at Didcot."

He was wrong there. For at the junction of the line a pointsman had made a mistake, and they all three went in three minutes through that door which I who am writing this and you who are reading it will have to pass.

It was a Death much more noisy and violent, but on the whole less painful, than most. There was a grinding and a heaving and a jarring, a little momentary sharp pain, then flames of which they did not feel the burning.

Their bodies, when these were recovered, could not be recognised by the features, but only by the clothes.

That of the squire was, I am glad to say, sent back to his native fields and buried in the same vault with his father and grandfather, who had been, to start with, a small moneylender in Hereford. That of the lawyer was buried down at his country place, where there were copper beeches and rhododendrons; also there was a memorial service for him at St. Margaret's, to which I was asked, but I did not go. The traveller was buried near by the accident: and why not? But they read a very nice paper about him at the Royal Geographical Society.

And of such is the kingdom of this world.

Bad News

I HAVE bad news for my colleagues in the detestable trade of writing. The novel is doomed. The novel, the easiest, the commonest, the flabbiest form, the least bounded, the least structural, the one most tempting men to mere babble and women to mere scrabble, is doomed.

The novel, in which the greatest writers of the modern interlude, of the revolutionary interlude, lying between the Encyclopedists and the Great War, delighted to engage their genius; the novel, achievement in which was the high road to glory; the novel which attached to one or two creative names each a universe of its own—so that Balzac, Schnifthausen, Dickens, Wolkau, Thackeray, Maciano, Scott, and I know not how many others whom I have not read, are attended like gods by creatures sprung from them alone and of their own devising—is doomed.

The novel, to which women ran as to a natural exercise and a natural food; the novel of which it may be said that no woman who could write a line in any language had not written at least one example; the novel which gave at once a new livelihood and a new pastime for the Sex—is doomed.

The novel, which came next after the daily press in its extended acreage of printed matter; the novel

66

which sprouted up increasing and increasing by the century, by the thousand, by the myriad; the novel which compelled those who sold it in bulk to hire vast rooms like warehouses wherein they stacked its enormous reservoirs—is doomed.

The novel, upon the basis of which your best-seller became not only a mighty prophet, but a firm authority upon theology, geology, morphology, tautology, history, mystery, defiance, alliance, physical science, politics and the æsthetic—is doomed.

Now what do you think of that? How does the future look to you now? Can you face it?

You the best-sellers (if you have made your investments prudently) need not trouble, and you that hardly make both ends meet on one miserable tale a year, will feel, I suppose, neither heat nor cold at this great news; for your lives are such that you hardly care whether your lives continue or no. But you, the vast army of young writers, who are just about to swash your bucketful of rubbish into this mighty existing sea of novels—the news must give *you* pause. You cannot write verse worth printing; you know nothing; you cannot think, you cannot construct a paragraph, you cannot pray, you cannot build, you cannot paint or draw, you cannot plough, you cannot ride a horse, you cannot handle a boat, you cannot solve an equation, you cannot draw up a sketch map, you cannot carpenter, you cannot work in metals. At least (you said) we can write novels. What then will you do when that one door is shut, as shut it is about to be? Sell shrimps perhaps. Yet am I doing you a service; for I am giving you warning while yet there is time. It may be five years, or a dozen, or even thirty. It is not appointed to you to know the times and the seasons. But the novel is doomed.

It is doomed as effectually as was doomed, round about the year of Waterloo, the English decasyllabic rhymed, heroic, iambic, didactic poem. It is doomed as surely as was doomed towards the year 1880 the evangelical treatise. It is doomed as surely as was doomed, not late in Queen Victoria's reign, the printed, the collected sermon. It is petering out; it is wobbling; it is on its last legs; it faints for breath; it has upon it those unmistakable signs which are the forerunners of the end; it has grown vapid; it has lost its norm; it gropes; it spreads its hands blindly; it is about to die.

No more shall undergraduates send their guineas to starving hacks that these may write a weekly essay for them to be read to the Master, comparing the novel and the drama as a form of expression. No longer shall the unhappy, the destitute, the isolated, the forsaken hack reviewers grind out week by week what their judgment is, their miserable judgment, upon the weekly pile of miserable fiction which they have not read. A little while, and no longer shall you hear that Miss Wilke has surpassed the greatest of her achievements or that Mr. Bilke has drawn the character of the charwoman with masterly reserve. A little while and it shall not be a question of sixty thousand words or of a hundred—for there will be none at all. A little while and the gambler's chance of a million sale will be a memory, like the memory of the largesse of the kings of old.

Do you imagine, as you read this revealed truth

68

from my pen, that posterity will pick up the old dead novel and browse in it here and there curiously, guessing how it was that we, the ancestors, could tolerate such stuff ? Do you think, do you dare to think, that I shall now bring out yet another of the ready-made phrases, and say that our descendants will "turn the pages" of *The Desert Lord*, of *Miriam's Mistake*, of *Evangel*, and ask themselves what on earth made such things tolerable at all? I shall use no words of the sort. Our descendants will not so browse; they will not so toy. Even before they have given up the unhealthy habit of perpetual reading; even before the knowledge of letters has been abandoned to a small, respected and (I hope) decently endowed class; even while there still remains some general practice of following printed matter, the dead corpse of the novel will be left abandoned and alone.

The very form will disgust our sons; the mere title, warning them that on some dusty shelf behind the binding lies that horrible thing a novel, will put them off with the violence of intolerable boredom. Here and there perhaps some novel, on the fly-leaf of which has been scribbled a piece of verse worth having or the name of some victorious general, its possessor, or the inscription of a lover, famous after death, will come into the auction room. But the novel as novel no one will touch with the tongs.

What then, you ask me, of the mountains of novels which now press down the earth ? How can such a mole be levelled ? At least the mere physical mass (you say) must remain.

You are wrong. That bulk of printed horror is but

part of a stream. It is like the water in the mill-dam, ever flowing out and ever renewed. That great, that best, that most beneficent of all modern machines, the Pulping Machine, destroys its countless novels year by year. As for the few that are not destroyed, these will disappear by the action of that same Mysterious Scavenger who (in what hours we know not, and by what means we know not) rids the earth of pins, old newspapers, dead cities and political reputations. None has seen this Angel, but we all witness his ceaseless care for the burdened generations of men. He, the Remover appointed of God, will sweep the remnants of all novels into his unseen, not earthly, bin.

But the great names, you ask me, the names which are now upon a par with the poets and the theologians and the soldiers of the world—these will remain? No, they won't. They will indeed survive their works by some few years; but not for very long, save such few as could achieve something more than novel-writing. The poets will survive, they are the toughest kind of meat for the teeth of Time; possibly the mathematicians will survive and certainly the theologians; but not the novelists, however garlanded. Their hour has struck, their business is at an end. And I, for one, rejoice.

Harold Hardrada, Poet

LOOK how the arts are all at one, and how true it
is that the Muses hold hands in a ring as they
dance round Apollo; whether he be weary of it
yet, I do not know. Even little Terpsichore,
of whom I am too fond, is not allowed to
break away. This truth occurred to me the other
morning, it reinvaded my mind, as I looked up the
authorities on the Battle of Stamford Bridge—
which was fought, you will remember (why should I
remind you? You are familiar with all these things!),
on September 25, 1066; a Monday; a very good day
on which to fight a battle; not desecrating the Sabbath
as did Waterloo, nor coming, like Hastings, at the end
of a tiresome week's work when something might be
lacking to the zest and spirit of the encounter.

Reading my authorities on Stamford Bridge I
discovered that history and lyric verse are in close
communion, and that art governs all.

For of authorities upon Stamford Bridge there is in
truth but one full and detailed, which is Snorro; and
Snorro's writing is not only itself poetic, but contains
the most delightful evidence of how poetry springs
up in the mind of man and especially in the mind of
the soldier, Harold Hardrada.

Even the duller authorities on Stamford Bridge,

71

who give us but a few lines of prose, cannot forbear the poetic mention of that one man holding the narrow bridge against a host until he was cut down. But Snorro out of Iceland, though writing an epic and writing a long time after, tells you the true story: it rings with truth; it is alive. Would that I could read that prose of his in his own tongue!

Therefore, have the dons blasphemed and called Snorro's story a myth because it is true. Better still, Snorro, himself a poet (and standing to the Battle as near as we stand to the American War of Independence), was himself inspired by the poems of his elders, which poems he had seen before his eyes and which he had himself copied, as he tells us. The first instinct of those men who took part in so vivid an affair was to express themselves in rhythm. It was the inspiration of verse which gave immortality to the fighting, which put life and pulsation into the record, which enshrined and crystallised and made permanent their experience. When they sang of those English horsemen riding round the ring of the Norwegian steel, difficult to front, they sang of things that they themselves had seen, felt, heard, enormously experienced; and I marvel that any miserable don, nearly a thousand years later born, should quaver out arguments against Englishmen having ridden horses in those days. Great heavens! When a man has stood up to a charge of horse, does he forget it? Does he mistake it for a charge of foot? Oh, Oxford, thou that sittest in the midst of the marshes and deceivest the very young! And Cambridge, too, for that matter.

But there is even more of poetry in that high story of

Stamford Bridge than the fact that its historian was a poet and that his authorities were the poets of his father's time who had talked with the fighting-men and with such few as escaped to make for the ships from the banks of the Derwent.

In the recital this splendid fellow remembers what all those soldiers also remember, the very noble custom of the time; which was that kings in arms, under the excitement and incitation of attack, should sing. And Harold Hardrada, when the English were upon him and he was about to swing his sword free of his mantle of blue, at once composed with great facility half-a-dozen lines of verse: not with a fountain pen miserably scratching out imitative stuff too late at night upon bad spirits, but in the open air of a Yorkshire morning, singing with his mouth (upon wine I hope) and having his weapon in his hand; watching the English as they came over the bridge and deployed, after they had broken down the resistance of the one hero who had held the narrow way.

Now note you this, Harold Hardrada was not of your gentlemen-poets who, writing for occasion and a little ashamed to be writing at all (thinking verse unworthy of a man of lineage and wealth), publish and confirm anything they may turn out and think the world should be only too grateful to have been given it. Far from it! Harold Hardrada did what all poets ought to do. When he had made up his nice little few lines of verse he turned to his companions-in-arms and he said, "I do not think those verses very good; I must better them." So, still with the English coming on, he made up another little poem and said, "That is much more satisfactory! That is much more the way in which the thing ought to be done!" And having so said, he turned to the business of fighting and fought all day, or rather, from the morning till noon, when an arrow caught him in the throat and he went down; worthy of his people and of so much fine sailing of the seas. He was a tall man, they say, but he had no contempt for short men: and when he saw the English herald, long before the battle, riding up he said, "This man is of low stature; but he sits well in his stirrups."

Indeed, all those men of old time, mixed struggle and every part of life with song. Nor were they the last; for a friend told me once that Frederick the Great, having been defeated in some action or other (this is not of my own reading, I only repeat it on hearsay), galloped away very rapidly with his secretary at his side, the secretary galloping I suppose more clumsily (for I suppose that secretary was not born with much wealth and therefore had not been bred to riding gentlemanly in his earlier years). When the king had ridden many, many miles and was safely away from his enemies, he drew rein and bade his unfortunate secretary set foot to ground, pull out his inkhorn, his pen and his paper and write; saying (so the tale was told me) "I have composed a fine set of verses upon a Defeated King—be good enough to take them down," which the secretary then did in that current French, which was the only language Frederick knew well, and in that abominable verse which so great, though wizened, a captain took for poetry: "He who looted so many towns and so many lines."

But really, when I come to think of it, few modern general officers, let alone kings, have set this supreme seal of verse upon their actions. I cannot recall one who wrote any poem at all upon his efforts during our recent troubles, and though the late King of Montenegro did write a poem upon the access of his little State to the Adriatic ("O Falcons of Tzernagora, the murmur of waves replies"), yet the practice of poetry has almost ceased to be a kingly art and has ceased to be a military art altogether. It will return.

One line lingers in my memory, speaking of the late war, and that is a line written by an English poet and printed in that repository of great verse, the *Times* newspaper, on the occasion of a naval action in the Bight of Heligoland, in the very first days of 1914. The line runs:—

"We bit them in the Bight!"

It haunts me! It haunts me still. . . .

Does anybody read nowadays I wonder the enthusiastic Roman verse upon the Battle of Pollentia? I doubt it. And I only wish we had similar verse about the capitulation of Fiesole. It would be much better evidence of what the early fifth century thought about the barbarians than anything else. Alaric was for them no more than a revolutionary Roman general who had mutinied with his troops and done great harm. But Fiesole, the destruction of myriads of barbarians, defeated as the barbarians always were when they attacked the might of Rome, cut to pieces by the hundred thousand, chained and sold for slaves at a Bradbury a head; *that* was a victory which the time understood and loved.

75

Now that so many anthologies are being published to the great profit of the publishers, to the small profit of the anthologists, and to the no-profit-at-all of the wretched poets themselves, why does not some publisher hire a starving man to make an anthology of battle-writing in verse?

It is, like all human achievement, one long triumphant progress from the lesser to the greater, from tentative barbaric origins to the full glory of our modern masters in English Rhyme.

There are passages in the Homeric poems not to be despised, and there is a chorus in the Hecuba asking how long it will be before the besiegers can get back home from Flanders—and so on through the ages. There is the song of Roland, and there is the song of Antioch, and there is Maldon, and there is Brunanburgh (of which Tennyson made a fine thing) and there is Chénier, and on and on it goes in a perpetually rising ecstasy of verse until we get that superlative, that culminating line, "We bit them in the Bight!"

To which finding nothing superior, I cease.

Lord Rumbo and Lord Jumbo

I.

Lord Rumbo was a Democrat
Who wore a very curious hat
And woollen boots, and didn't think
It right to smoke or take a drink.

II.

He also thought it rather wrong
To hum the chorus of a song.
But what he simply couldn't stand
Was Billiard Tables off the Strand.

III.

Yes! Billiard Tables off the Strand!
Lord Jumbo, on the other hand,
Was quite another sort of cove.
What? Yes by God!—and also Jove.

IV.

He was a Tory thick and thin.
His hat was made of Beaver Skin.
He practised every kind of sport
And drank a dreadful deal of Port.

V.

Etc. ——

LORD RUMBO was devoted to the cause of Democracy. He passionately desired the determination of International Difficulties by Peaceful Conference conducted through Parliamentarians who should be chosen by other Parliamentarians (or by themselves) for that office. Though doubtful whether the populace should be

77

directly consulted upon matters concerning them, he made no doubt that they should all be given a vote for the election of men and women who, once elected, should make what laws they pleased. He judged that the boundaries of national feeling were best discovered by those of language, with which they were coterminous; and he could conceive nothing worse in the ordering of mankind than a popular monarchy —or, indeed, personal rule of any sort.

Certain minor questions, such as the indissolubility of marriage, the right to property, and so forth, he delighted to leave to open discussion, and he was wont to observe that all men should be absolutely free to act, write, speak, and think as they pleased within the limits of the law, whatever that law might be. If he made certain exceptions to this general doctrine (as, of bigamy in Utah, or the sect known as Thugs in India), they were so slight as not to blemish the stainless purity of his principles.

He had long discovered that the use of Leathern footwear was both cruel and disgusting; cruel because it was provided by the hide of a hapless brother animal which had done us no wrong; and disgusting for reasons upon which he was too refined to dwell. He was, therefore, used to wear woollen boots, which gave him a very striking and individual appearance. He also wore a hat of some strange shape, but this he did not put on in order to attract attention so much as from a strongly marked personality which naturally stamped itself upon everything about him.

His religion was of the most exalted and abstracted type, purged of all concrete dross and reposing only upon the reverent and rational exercise of man's moral nature; but the smoking of tobacco, which he recognised as a grave social evil, he constantly opposed. He was still more emphatic in his condemnation of wine, beer and spirits, since it could not be denied that, upon analysis, these were found to contain *alcohol ;* so exact and unwarped was his intellectual process that he put upon the same plane of condemnation, a Richebourg of 1906 and that potato spirit which, having been distilled by the efficient German scientists of Hamburg, is conveyed under our flag to the natives of Nigeria.

He was further moved to protest against those popular songs which succeed each other so rapidly in the public mouth, and which are, at the worst coarse, and at the best, inane. In turn "Two Lovely Black Eyes," "Tarrarra-Boomde-ay," "Hiawatha," "Tipperary," and "It is not going to Rain any more" received his severe reproof, which he had the courage to utter in public when anybody was so rash as to hum the offensive notes.

But since every man of energy and conviction must, if he is to obtain a particular success, in some degree circumscribe his effort to one object, Lord Rumbo directed many years of strenuous and at last successful labour toward the restriction, and, as he hoped, the abolition, of the game of billiards; particularly as it was played in haunts neighbouring the Strand and Charing Cross. For he was a pioneer in this matter, and he perceived, long before the general public had woken up to so vital a truth, that the pushing of an ivory ball, whether red or white, with the end of a

79

long thin stick, was ruinous to proper morals, to the well-being of Society, and, indeed, to the Spirit of the Gospel.

Such was Lord Rumbo, a living proof that a man may be an English gentleman and yet a Radical.

Lord Jumbo, his cousin, was a man of very different stamp. Though closely connected in blood (the third Lord Rumbo and the fifth Lord Jumbo having married sisters, to wit, Lady Amelia and Lady Caroline), and commonly addressing the one the other by the familiar terms of "Ricky" and "Nibs," there was an irreconcilable contrast in temper, and therefore in political theory, between the two men.

Lord Jumbo affected the dress and manner of an earlier period. He wore, till others had long discarded it, that kind of hat known as a Beaver; he loved to be seen in a pink coat with leather breeches and top boots, and would hold in his right hand a short whip handle adorned with a prodigiously long lash, which he carried curled up and firmly grasped. Dogs were his delight; and many, of various breeds, would loyally accompany him in his walks abroad.

He hunted the fox with varying success, shot accurately at fowls expensively preserved for the purpose, and was not above running, in spite of his advancing age, after beagles in pursuit of the hare. He loudly proclaimed his attachment to roast beef, the Hanoverian dynasty (and, indeed, this was well established), the National flag and the principle of an Indissoluble Union with Ireland: in which last conviction he remains unshaken, I am glad to say, to this day. Of the many beverages he consumed, port was his most familiar, and the most consonant with his character and frame; and so expert was he in its consumption that he could readily distinguish between the vintage of Islington and the more expensive product of Peninsular origin. He loved to address his fellow subjects from the platform at political meetings and never failed, at the inception of each address, to proclaim his ignorance of book learning and to say that he pretended to no special talents—in which declaration he was warmly supported by all who heard him.

He was of opinion that the natural rulers of the country were himself, and this led him to a great indulgence towards those who were of his own way of thinking, but, also, I am sorry to say, to a touch of intolerance against those who might presume to be of another.

He could never clearly understand why a heavy duty was not levied at the ports upon wheat, and, indeed, upon every other kind of agricultural produce; for it was clear to him that such an impost would raise the price of crops (save possibly roots and hay) and would thus benefit not only the farmers, but also the landlords of England. This hankering of his for a more expensive loaf was, perhaps, his chief disagreement with the bulk of his fellow subjects, who none the less respected, and even loved him, as typical of themselves in their traditional aspect just as they respected and loved his cousin, Lord Rumbo, as typical of themselves in the sterner moral inheritance of their blood.

By a beautiful dispensation of Providence it had

F

been vouchsafed that the People of England should be ruled alternately, first by Lord Rumbo and then by Lord Jumbo; so that their emoluments, towards the close of a useful public career, should amount to much the same sum and their savings upon such salaries to a comfortable fortune and provision for their descendants. Nor can it be denied that this simple constitution worked with excellent effect throughout a nation united in a common and vigorous patriotism, supreme in trade and in maritime affairs, good humoured, courageous, and of a spontaneous ingenuity which was the despair of rivals.

So things would have continued for ever had there not come a day in 1914 when. . . .

Talking of Domesday

I HAVE just spent a solid day and a half upon Domesday Book for a little piece of historical writing I am doing, and during that session two things on which my mind has turned incessantly for the last twenty-five years struck me once more with such force that I cannot let them sleep in my mind, but am compelled by the Daemon to write of them.

The first of these is the way in which some particular doctrine in history becomes fixed and, as it were, official, so that a man challenging it is in a worse position than was ever any heretic. The second is the curious distaste our Universities have for common sense: reality.

Now I don't suggest that these two little troubles are at all new. Ever since teaching began, and ever since learned men delighted in research and hypothesis, that is, from at least the beginning of civilised record, these two features of academic life, an official doctrine and a horror of reality, must have been present, and in a dozen cases we know that they were present. The history of official academics is a procession of such errors, each petrifying and each only to be blasted out after a lengthy bombardment.

What *is*, perhaps, novel is the degree in which we

suffer from those vices to-day—although, as is always the case when intellectual disease is at its worst, the patients ignore it.

There is not one academic man in a hundred who would admit that here in England to-day official academic doctrine on anything is more rigid than ever it was in the past, or that neglect of common sense is more advanced in his world than ever it was in the past. But it is so. And the progress of the spirit which makes it so has been evident throughout the whole of my lifetime, and I think throughout the better part of the nineteenth century.

Perhaps the explanation is that when men lose divine doctrine, they must construct dogmas of their own making to take its place and to satisfy the appetite for security: so they accept the authority of print and what they hope to be a purely rational process behind the print. Or, perhaps, it is the prodigious advance of physical science discovering, one after another, a thousand new truths which are supported by the absolute proof of repeated experiment. Such a triumph in one department of human knowledge naturally affects all others.

Modern men know that if they deny some new conquest of physical science, they will be making fools of themselves; and the examples of those who do attempt such denials is a dreadful warning. For what every man most dreads is making a fool of himself.

Perhaps the cause of the modern dogmatism and the modern dislike of reality is the recent rapid multi-plication of the categories of knowledge. This increase in the number of separate studies has rendered timid

84

the person of common culture, whose judgment is the best corrective of extravagance. The average educated man who would not have hesitated to inquire upon a matter of general interest two generations ago is now terrified of the expert. And when a man knows that his fellows are terrified of him he always goes off the rails.

Whatever the cause, there the thing undoubtedly is.

In the particular case of Domesday, I find it in the matter of population; the guesses at the total population of England at the turn of the eleventh and twelfth centuries. There has arisen a rooted dogma that the population of England up to the present borders of Scotland and Wales was something under two million. The truth is that the numbers were anything from twice to three times that amount. But I have only to assert that truth in so simple a form to be certain that the few who do me the honour to read me will at once set me down for an extravagant fool at the best, and an insincere or perverse one at the worst; which shows how right I am in saying that academic dogmas to-day have a better anchor-hold than ever they had in the past. For not one in a thousand of those who judge thus has even glanced at the evidence, or knows by what process the error has arisen. It has arisen from a neglect of common sense; from an exaggerated reliance upon a document and guess-work on it, uncorrected by general considerations.

The number of individuals, presumably adult males (but one or two women among them) mentioned in the Survey of 1086, would come, extended to the whole country, to roughly 300,000. The doctrine has arisen that these represent all the heads of families; if you take six for the number of souls represented by one family, and certain frills possibly omitted in the survey, it is a most generous multiple, a maximum one; and therefore the total population would be roughly 1,800,000.

I take it that a sensible reading of the evidence, that is, a reading played upon by a general knowledge of men and things, shows quite clearly that in Domesday we are not dealing with heads of families at all; we are dealing with some now forgotten and very imperfectly understood system of assessment towards one particular income, and only one, to wit, the King's income. We know what the arable area of England normally is. It is about 10,000,000 acres, and that feeds easily 6,000,000 and may support much more than 6,000,000 souls. The famous estimate made at the end of the seventeenth century gave us such figures, and we know that, allowing for the improvement in agriculture which immediately followed, those figures are true to-day. We know that before the industrial revolution the structure of the country had remained stable for centuries. We can, of course, allow for some clearing and draining under the organising energy of the Middle Ages, and especially during the great development of the thirteenth century; but then England had been a properly civilised Christian State for many generations before the Conquest, and even the arable land mentioned in the Inquisition of 1086 does not fall far short of this pivot number of 10,000,000 acres: It gives 8,000,000 for the imperfect area surveyed.

86

If you turn from that to the negative argument, it is equally strong. You can take almost any excerpt at random in Domesday itself or in the Cambridge Inquisitions, which are more detailed, and come to the same conclusion—to wit, that the names mentioned are not a census nor anything approaching a census.

Common sense will tell you, or in the lack of it, a very few months' experience, that you cannot plough the land and manure it and harrow it and sow it and reap it and mow it and stack and thrash with flails, and milk your cows and see to the calving and to the stalling of your cattle, and to carting, and to weeding and cleaning, and at the same time weave, spin, build, fence, ditch, keep roads, hew timber, quarry stone, man ships, carry goods, all that with one man to each arable 20 acres. Our University men talk nonsense with a unanimity and an assurance quite novel, and they are worst of all when they talk false history. For false history is necessary to false philosophy. You might as well try and run a 300-ton ship with a steward, a mate and a boy; and yet it is all that the census idea of Domesday would give you.

Or look at almost any entry. You get less than 1,000 priests mentioned in all England—an England in which there were by tradition 20,000 village units, and even by the admission of the worst pedants, not less than 8,000. You get ten shepherds for the whole of Sussex! And exactly three quarries in the same unhappy county; and exactly three people to say Mass for the whole population. You get any number of miraculous men turned loose upon 60 acres of arable with not a soul to help them. You get Bosham, a port then of importance, with no sailors, no shipyards, and no ships; you get four mills, but no millers, etc., etc., etc.

It won't work. It is nonsense.

Is it, then, of any value to attack such nonsense? Yes; in the long run you drag out the rooted error and history breathes again.

Is it worth an individual's while to make the challenge?

Most emphatically—NO.

Talking (Yet Again) of Fools

I HAVE written on the Fool all my life and once I lectured on Fools—in the schools at Oxford, of all places in the world. It was in connection with Rabelais. But there is no end to the subject, so I may boldly return to it. I was set to work by reading in a newspaper to-day a certain piece of advice which the writer said was given by Lord Chesterfield, to wit, that one should always speak to Fools in plain terms whether of truth or lies, since they are angered and bewildered by any form of subtlety and by irony most of all.

In all my long meditations upon Fools and my observation of them in many climates, I had not thought of this. I now see it to be true and the new truth illuminates me; it makes me understand many a quarrel and misunderstanding in my life. But that piece of advice is only one of a very great number of proverbs, epigrams and judgments upon the Fool which have accumulated through the ages and have not yet been got together, co-ordinated, digested into a Monograph upon the Fool.

I perpetually regret that I have not the years remaining, nor the energy, nor the leisure to write any one of these books which my mind as perpetually suggests to me; one of them would be this great Monograph upon the Fool.

I would issue it in two large volumes costing one guinea each, so that the whole book should be at 42s. net. There would be a great number of portraits of Fools, both living and dead, and composite photographs and diagrams, and statistics, and curves, and tests. Then, towards the end, I would have a practical division of how to entreat and nurture the Fool, just as books on Rainbow Trout and Hampshire Hogs have a section showing you how you ought to deal with these animals. In this practical part of the book (where most of the many proverbs would be collected) I would have a careful table of expenses showing you how the Fool may be used for profit, just as one is shown how to make a fowl farm pay. Indeed, this part of the book might be called "The Fool for Profit or Pleasure." Then I would have sections by experts on the Fool in different foreign countries and there would be an historical section on the Fools of the Past; but this historical section I should certainly hand over to an amateur, for I am afraid the University Historians would think they were having their legs pulled and a certain fellow feeling might make them refuse to lend a hand.

The real trouble of such a Monograph would be the difficulty of definition, because men are not perfectly agreed as to what the Fool may be. In my suggestion (made some years back) for the production of a *Cad's Encyclopædia*, the matter was easier; for the Cad is a generally recognised type. But the trouble about the

90

Fool is that men differ upon his character, they differ upon the tests by which you may know him; and they do so upon this account, that for each of us a Fool is one who has no aptitude for some use of the mind which we think important; but we differ as to what uses of the mind we think important, and therefore we differ in our definitions of the Fool.

To one large important section of society, that which is engaged in accumulating money, the mark of the Fool is an inability to keep money. But to another large body of educated men, it is rather the other way, and a pre-occupation with money is regarded as a symptom of folly. Everyone who is an adept at some physical exercise secretly thinks those to be Fools who practise it, but practise it indifferently; the idea being that they ought to know beforehand whether they are good at the thing or not, and that if they are not that they ought to leave it alone; that no one has a right to touch the sacred sport for personal amusement, but only as a proof of excellence. This is especially true of shooting.

Talkativeness is a mark of a Fool to one set of men, and (surprising though it sounds to our generation) obstinate silence is certainly the mark of a Fool to another set of men. An inability to follow one particular kind of jest is the mark of a Fool in those who admire that kind of jest. But kinds of jests differ; they differ more almost than any other set of spiritual categories.

For instance, I myself have heard with my own ears Englishmen say that in Scotland men had no sense of humour! Yet nowhere out of Scotland have I heard true humour on those Infernal Twins, Sin and Death.

And, lastly, you get the bewildering truth that two individuals may be so contrasted that each looks like a Fool to the other; and the thought of that is known as "The Fool's Consolation"; all Fools in their secret hearts cherish the truth that they are only seeming Fools in others' eyes, but in the sight of heaven are most gifted.

The Fool in Scripture is opposed to the Wise Man rather than to the Intelligent Man, and if Scripture be inspired (as so many still stoutly maintain), and may be taken as an ultimate court of appeal, we may say that the Fool is not the opposite of the man who appreciates irony and mystery and can think clearly, but the opposite of the man who understands the things of heaven and earth; whose judgments are in general sound and who directs his life towards the right ends.

If this be the true definition of the Fool (and it seems to me, I confess, upon the whole the best) then Carlyle's one tolerable sentence would be true, not only of his fellow subjects, but of the whole world. For it is manifest that most men direct their lives with little judgment, tested by no matter what standard you like to take. Knowing perfectly well what the consequences of certain acts will be, and being perfectly ready to admit that these consequences are especially to be avoided, yet are men found in the practice of these actions perpetually; they are found repeating them after, not mere warnings, but burning experience. The Fool, then, above all things, lacks proportion, and gives the wrong values to things, and gets them in the wrong order; or at any rate comes upon them in the wrong order. But here it seems to me that one should distinguish between the Fool in action and the Fool in spirit, for a man may be very wise in his judgments and exact in his sense of proportion, and yet in action yield perpetually to appetites or sloths which he admits to be his ruin.

I think that when we talk of the Fool we nearly always mean the Fool in spirit and not the Fool in action.

I have often and long considered whether political and social ambition were marks of a Fool, and I have decided at last that they are.

The ambition for real power is no mark of the Fool—it is justified though it leads to Hell. A man who enjoys real power (such power as is given to-day by wealth and was, long ago, by courage) will tell you that a satisfaction of this appetite for power is, to him, well worth the price he pays for it.

But in all times social ambition, the ambition to be thought important in a vague, not a specific way, in some way not attaching to one's own personality or achievement, but to a sort of general illusion, is surely folly. It is paying solid money or solid comfort for something emptier than mist, and it has this further element of folly about it that it is never satisfied.

To-day what we call political ambition—ambition to attain certain titular ranks in public life—has fallen into the same category. There is very little real power left attached to such positions; such labels as "Prime Minister," "Secretary for Foreign Affairs," have come very close to being mere social titles. We already admit that a man who wants to be called Privy Councillor and write Right Honourable before his name and drop the esquire after it, wants a purely social distinction. There is no power about it whatsoever. Two hundred and fifty years ago there was a great deal of power attached to the post, and three hundred years ago there was more power attached to it than there is to-day to a great financier or the owner of a great newspaper in England or to the head of an armed force among the Germans. But to-day it has no power left at all, and the other political titles are rapidly going the same way. You cannot say of the holder of any one of them, not even of the holder of the highest, that he is not much more afraid of financial power, or the power of publicity, than the holders of those powers are afraid of him. Yet both social ambition and its close cousin, political ambition, still lead men to the complete topsyturvydom of Fools—to the buying of 4d. for 9d. all the time; to a mug's game.

There is in this common sort of folly something of what you find in a lottery: £100,000 are paid in to a lottery which yields only £1,000 as a prize. Yet you will easily kid 100,000 men to give a £1 each for their chance of that £1,000 prize. Men buy a thing at 100 times its right value because the difference between their £1 risked and their possible £1,000 gained is so large that they cannot calculate it; it seems to them like an infinity.

How generously has Providence behaved to the Fool! No animal has been granted a stronger faculty for self-preservation. The Fool learns from child-

94

hood to put on a mask of pomposity or cunning. He learns discretion in speech, restraint in gesture, and we can all bear witness that the startling Fools, the great Master Fools of our experience, have been men whose folly was only discovered late; appearing suddenly; piercing through.

Last, let this be remembered; that any man attempting a definition of Fools discovers himself in the process to be a Fool, and I verily believe that this book of mine on Fools, which I have been planning, had best be left to be written by a Fool, and some day I will leave directions for posterity, showing how such an author should be selected.

Talking (and Singing) of the Nordic Man

I.
Behold, my child, the Nordic man,
And be as like him as you can:
His legs are long, his mind is slow,
His hair is lank and made of tow.

II.
And here we have the Alpine Race:
Oh! what a broad and brutal face!
His skin is of a dirty yellow.
He is a most unpleasant fellow

III.
The most degraded of them all
Mediterranean we call.
His hair is crisp, and even curls,
And he is saucy with the girls.

THIS translation is my own. I offer it with diffidence, for I recognise that it does not reproduce the deep organ tones of the original. But it gives the substance of that fine poem, and it is only with the substance—I mean that description of The Race which it conveys—that I have here to deal.

I heard so much about the Nordic Man in these last few months that I was moved to collect recently a great mass of information upon him and to coordinate it. Upon the Alpine Man and the Mediterranean Man I am not so erudite: nor is it indeed to any great purpose that I should be—for they are clearly inferior. But the Nordic Man is worth anybody's trouble; and here is what I have found out about him.

He is the Conqueror and the Adventurer. He is the Lawgiver and the essentially Moral Man. He arranges the world as it should be arranged. He does everything for his own good and for the good of others. He is a Natural Leader. Even those who hate him, fear him; all respect him. The Alpine Man sits sullenly at his feet awaiting his orders; the Mediterranean Man flies in terror from his face.

But it is not enough to learn these general characters in the Nordic Man, pleasing though they are. No sound biologist could be content until he knew something intimate of his origin and habits; where he may be found, what he does, and how to tell him at sight.

This, then, is what I have found about the Nordic Man. I have space only for the most salient points, but I hope to complete the picture in detail when I shall have leisure to write my book on the species. It will be fully illustrated and will have a very complete Index.

The Nordic Man is born either in the West End of London or in a pleasant country house, standing in its own park-like grounds. That is the general rule; he is, however, sometimes born in a parsonage and rather more frequently in a Deanery or a Bishop's Palace, or a Canon's house in a Close. Some of this type have been born in North Oxford; but none (that I can discover) in the provincial manufacturing towns, and certainly none east of Charing Cross or south of the river.

The Nordic Man has a nurse to look after him while he is a baby, and she has another domestic at her service. He has a night and a day nursery, and he is full of amusing little tricks which endear him to his parents as he grows through babyhood to childhood.

Towards the age of ten or eleven, the Nordic Man goes to a preparatory school, the headmaster of which is greatly trusted by the Nordic Man's parents, especially by the Nordic Man's mother. He early learns to Play the Game, and is also grounded in the elements of Good Form, possibly the Classics and even, exceptionally, some modern tongue. He plays football and cricket; usually, but not always, he is taught to swim.

Thence the Nordic Man proceeds to what is called a Public School, where he stays till he is about eighteen. He then goes either to Oxford or Cambridge, or into the Army. He does not stay long in the Army; while from the University he proceeds either to a profession (such as the Bar, or writing advertisements) or to residence upon his estate. This last he can only do if his father dies early.

The Nordic Man lives in comfort and even luxury through manhood; he shoots, he hunts, he visits the South of France, he plays bridge. He hates the use of scent; he changes for dinner into a special kind of clothes every day. He is extremely particular about shaving, and he wears his hair cut short and even bald. The Nordic does not bother much about Religion, so when he approaches death he has to distract himself

98

with some hobby, often that of his health. He dies of all sorts of things, but more and more of the cancer; after his death his sons, nephews or cousins take up the rôle of the Nordic Man and perpetuate the long and happy chain.

Such is the life-story of the Nordic Man. I have only given it in its broadest lines, and have left out a great many sub-sections; but what I have said will be sufficient to indicate places in which he is to be surprised and the kind of things which you will there find him doing. As for his character, which lies at the root of all this great performance, that is less easily described, for one might as well attempt to describe a colour or a smell; but I can attempt some indications of it.

The Nordic Man dislikes all cruelty to animals, and is himself kind to them in the following scale: first the dog, then the horse, then the cat, then birds, and so on till you get to insects, after which he stops caring. Microbes, oddly enough, he detests. He will treat them in the most callous manner.

In the matter of wine the Nordic Man is divided; you cannot predicate of him that he will drink it, or that if he drinks it he will know what it is. But in the matter of whisky you may safely say that it is his stand-by, save for a certain sub-section of him who dare not touch it. These stand apart and are savage to their fellows.

The Nordic Man is very reserved, save in the matter of speech-making. He hates to betray an emotion, but he hates still more the complete concealment of it. He has therefore established a number of conventions whereby it may be known when he is angry, pleased or what not; but he has no convention for fear, for he is never afraid. This reminds me that the Nordic Man despises conflict with lethal weapons unless it be against the enemies of his country; but he delights in watching, and will sometimes himself practise, conflict conducted with stuffed gloves. As for fighting with his feet, he would not dream of it; nor does he ever bite.

The Nordic Man is generous and treats all men as his equals, especially those whom he feels to be somewhat inferior in rank and wealth. This is a very beautiful trait in the Nordic Man, and causes him to believe that he is everywhere beloved. On the other hand, the Nordic Man prefers to live with those richer than himself. The Nordic Man detests all ostentation in dress, and detests even more the wearing of cheap clothes. He loves it to be known that his clothes were costly. No Nordic Man wears a made-up tie.

The Nordic Man boasts that he is not addicted to the Arts, and here he is quite right; but he is an excellent collector of work done by the inferior Mediterranean race, and is justly proud of the rare successes of his own people in this field. In the same way the Nordic Man will tell you with emphasis that he cannot write. Herein he tells the truth. Yet, oddly enough, he is convinced that no one has ever been able to write except Nordic Men; and this article of faith he applies particularly to True Poetry, which (he conceives) can only be inspired in his own tongue.

The Nordic Man does everything better than anybody else does it, and himself proclaims this truth unceasingly; but where he particularly shines is in the administration of justice. For he will condemn a man to imprisonment or death with greater rapidity than will the member of any other race. In giving judgment he is, unlike the rest of the human species, unmoved by any bias of class or blood, let alone of personal interest. On this account his services as a magistrate are sought far and wide throughout the world, and his life is never in danger save from disappointed suitors or those who have some imaginary grievance against him.

The Nordic Man is a great traveller. He climbs mountains; he faces with indifference tropical heat and arctic cold. He is a very fine fellow.

I must conclude by telling you all that I am not obtaining these details from any personal observations, as the part of the country in which I live has very few Nordic Men, and most of them are away during the greater part of the year staying either in the houses of other Nordic Men or in resorts of ritual pleasure upon the Continent. But I have had the whole thing described to me most carefully by a friend of mine who was for a long time himself a Nordic Man, until he had the misfortune to invest in British Dyes and crashed. He guarantees me the accuracy of his description.

*   *   *   *   *   *

Immediately after I had written those few words you have just read about the Nordic Man, I received a great quantity of letters from—I was about to write "from all quarters of the world," when I suddenly remembered that there would not be time for that, and that the lie would stick out—a great quantity of letters,

I say, from all sorts of people. It shows at once how widely I am read, and what interest my handling of this great subject aroused.

Some of these letters are abusive, some laudatory, some critical; all three categories are to me sacred when the writers have the courage to give name and address, and I would not divulge to the public the confidences they contain. But I think I may be allowed to answer here such correspondents as refused to give name and address. They will serve as examples to show how little the true doctrine of the Nordic Man has, so far, penetrated the masses.

Of course it will soak through at last, as all great scientific truths do—such as the doctrine of Natural Selection and the peculiar properties of the stuff called Ether, not to speak of Magna Charta, which even the poorest scavenger in the street to-day reveres as the origin of his freedom.

But so far this new discovery of the Nordic Man has not spread as it should have done.

Thus the first of my correspondents (who signs "Gallio" and gives no address but Brighton) is puzzled by the apparent aptitude of the Romans in their best period for administration and government, and even, in a primitive fashion, for war. He admits that all this may be much exaggerated, and from what he has seen of the Romans (he was down among them lately) he cannot believe all he hears of their ancestors. But still (he supposes) there must be a solid kernel of truth in it; for after all, the name "Roman" was given to a great number of institutions—including the Empire itself— and he asks me—rather crudely—how this was possible if the Mediterranean race were as vile as our greatest authorities have discovered it to be? It is odd that the simple answer to this difficulty has not occurred to the writer. It is that those who governed the Empire, and led the armies, called "Roman" were Nordic. This could be proved in several ways, but all of them might be open to objection save the unanswerable one that if these men had not been Nordic they could not have succeeded as they did. The Scipios, the Julian House, Hadrian—to cite at random—were manifestly and necessarily Nordic: for men do not act as they acted unless they are of pure bred Nordic stock.

The same is true of other manifestations of intelligence and vigour in Mediterranean countries. Thus the Italians and even the Greeks have left a considerable body of remarkable literature both in prose and in verse, and in the case of Italy, we have even quite modern examples of literary excellence—at least, so I am assured by those who are acquainted with the idioms of the inferior races. But upon examination it will always be found that the authors, though using a base medium, were Nordic. The committee which we collectively call by the mythological term "Homer," and which drew up and passed certainly the Iliad and possibly the Odyssey, were clearly Nordic in composition. Catullus was as Nordic as he could be. The Nordic character of Aristotle is a commonplace. Dante was Nordic. So was Leopardi.

Take any outstanding Italian or other Mediterranean name and you will find upon close examination that the man to whom it is attached was of the Nordic type: Napoleon Buonaparte occurs at once to the mind.

Another correspondent has come upon the thing from a different angle. He knows enough of the great new discovery to understand the term "cephalic index," and he has had his own cephalic index taken by a cephalogian who practises in Ealing. He did so under the impression, of course, that he was of sound Nordic stock; but to his horror the measurements have come out an extreme form of Alpine! He asks me what he is to do about it? I can assure him (and though I do not claim to be an expert in Morono-vitalogy I am fairly well up in my elements) that his anxiety is groundless. Though, of course, skull measurement is the basis of the three great divisions, yet if a man have Nordic qualities clearly apparent in his birth and culture, these easily predominate over what might be the natural tendencies of brachy-cephalic humanity. It would be a fine state of things, indeed, if we had to rule out of the Nordic excellence all those great men of the English past who, so far as we can judge from their portraits, had something flat-headed about them.

A third correspondent—who signs her letter "Onyx"—is troubled about her children. There are five: three charming boys and two delightful girls. She has measured their heads with her husband's calipers (he is an architect in full employment) and she finds that her eldest and her youngest are quite un-mistakably Mediterranean; her second eldest pain-fully Alpine, only her second youngest clearly Nordic; while the one in the middle, a boy (by name, she tells

104

me, Ethelred), seems to be a strange mixture of all three.

I cannot reply personally to this correspondent, as she does not give an address; but I trust that these lines will meet her eye. I would have her note that in the first place the skulls of children are no index to the shape they will have when they fossilise in mature years; and next, that even if these varied types appear in her family, it is not remarkable, for all three types are present in England. Moreover, she may have travelled.

A fourth correspondent, a clergyman, I fancy, who signs "Scholasticus," writes me a long rigmarole (I cannot call it by any politer name), in which he calls the whole theory subversive of sound morals, and asks whether we are to believe that man "created in the image of his Maker, and responsible to his Creator," etc., etc., etc.

Really, to this kind of thing there is only one answer. Science does not clash with religion; it clashes with nothing except unreason and untruth. Science is simply organised knowledge, based upon experiment and accurate measurement over so wide a field as to be established with absolute certitude. Now Science clearly proves that these three races, the Nordic, the Alpine, and the Mediterranean, exist side by side in Europe, and affirms that the Nordic (to which all scientific men belong) possesses those qualities upon which alone men can pride themselves. Science demonstrates the defects and vices of the Alpine, and the baseness and degradation of the Mediterranean stock. If my reverend critic likes to knock his head against a stone wall, I cannot help it. But it seems to me an extraordinary thing to find any man possessed of enough education to write consecutively, opposing (at this time of day) established scientific truths in the name of hypothetical principles, the figments of imagination and vanity. His "Creator," "image," "responsibility," are all of them mere words; not one of them has been established by accurate and repeated measurement, nor have they one single experiment conducted under scientific conditions to support them; while on the other side we have the unanimous agreement of Meyerbath, Karsowitz, Brahmsohn, Farrago, Cent-Six, Blauwvenfeld, Tabouche, Smith of Milwaukee (Hamilcar Q. Smith—perhaps the greatest authority of all), van Houten and his famous relative Klotz—but why should I prolong the list? My objector will look in vain through all the distinguished ranks of modern science to find a single name supporting his ridiculous assumptions of a "God," "Free Will" and what not. All agree that our characters and actions proceed from a cephalic index, and all are agreed upon the relative values of the three main races of Europe.

P.S.—To my correspondent "Tiny," who has also given no address, I must reply in this brief postscript. No, the facial angle, as measured from the point of the chin tangentially, the parietal curve of the forehead, and from the cusp of the left nostril to the base of the corresponding ear-lobe, is no longer the criterion of character. I thought I had made that plain. Thirty-five years ago, when I was a boy, all scientists were agreed that the facial angle was the one certain and only test of moral attitude and intellectual power; but that opinion is now universally abandoned, and the facial angle is replaced by the cephalic index.

So put that in your pipe and smoke it.

A Conversation with a Reader

PEOPLE whose books sell largely (mine do not, I am sorry to say—but perhaps some day they will) must often have had an experience which only came to me once in my life: that of talking familiarly with a member of the public who was reading one of my immortal works. But I cannot remember anyone who has given the world an account of such an experience. I will take the opportunity of doing so here; for it still gives me perpetual pleasure and amusement.

It is now many years ago. I was travelling down from Birmingham to London on the Great Western Railway. I was in a third-class smoking carriage with one other person, whom I took (from his little black bag and his manner) to be a commercial traveller, but he may have been anything else, a publican or the Hangman. He had a good solid face, and rather a fine one; strong hands, and a quiet demeanour. It was in the early autumn and sunny weather—such weather prepared me to be contented with the world and any chance companion. My heart was already high, when it rose dizzily upon my catching the title of the book which my fellow-traveller had in his hand. It was one of my too numerous books of essays.

I thought to myself "This is fame; I am getting

known. This man is a very good specimen of the average public. I love him; he is reading my book. Doubtless many hundreds up and down the great enchanted island are doing the same, some reading one book, some another. They will read and re-read these books until their covers are worn out, and then they will buy another copy. They will tell their friends. More and more copies will sell. The world has changed its complexion and my sun has risen at last."

As these pleasing thoughts succeeded each other in my mind the man opposite me put down the volume with a sigh (or, to be more particular, chucked it down on the dirty cushion), looked up to me and said, "Silly stuff that."

I said, "Yes," and asked him how he came to read it.

He said, "I dunno," and looked calmly at nothing for a short space in silence.

Then he added, "I was just looking over the book-stall and the man recommended it to me. I think he must have taken it up by mistake for another book. Anyhow, it's a shilling wasted" (for in those days the cheap editions were at a shilling).

I asked him who the author was, and he again said dully, "I dunno." But he made a languid gesture, picked up the book again, looked at the back, pronounced my name wrongly, and then threw the book down again—and once more sighed.

"Funny thing," he said, "this idea of reading when one's travelling; but I have got so that I must read something—only I can't read *that* stuff."

This time there was a note of bitterness in his complaint. I do not think he would have felt so strongly about it if he had found the poor little volume lying about; it was having spent a shilling on it that rankled.

I said, "What's it all about?"

"I dunno," he answered. "Nothing that I can make out!"

He picked up the book again and looked at the title. "It doesn't tell you on the outside. What they've printed there is just foolishness. There's no story I can make out. It's all cut up. Might be newspaper articles!"

All these words of his were painful ones. They were indeed newspaper articles which I, poor hack, had strung together, and put between covers for my living.

"Anyhow," he went on, in the slightly more interested tone of a man who wants to begin a conversation, "it beats me why people want to publish books like that!"

I said, "It was probably done for money." He repeated, "Seems so; but there can't be much in it." Then he said, "Never heard of him before!" and looked out of the window sadly, and added, "And don't want to hear of him again!"

I asked him who were his favourite authors. He mentioned several, to repeat whose names would, I suppose, be libel; one of them was a poet. It gave me pleasure to think that the man read verse, and I asked him what it was he liked about this poet. He suddenly became enthusiastic.

"It's splendid stuff," he said; "good ringing stuff! None of your little England about it!" and he recited the Poem called "Has made us what we are."

"That's the stuff!" he said, and added "to give 'em."

Then after a pause, "It stirs the blood." He was prepared to affirm that there was nothing the matter with old England so long as stuff like that could be written.

Then he started another kind of poem by the same man. This time it was all about a dear little child. It was called "Sambo's Prayer." When he had finished he sighed. Then he said with a kind of quizzical look, as though examining the depths of his heart, "I wonder how it comes to 'em? It's genius, I suppose. You and I couldn't do that." He shook his head, "No, not for a handful of golden sovereigns we couldn't! It just comes to 'em."

I asked him if he had ever met the Great Poet, but he said, "Lord, no!" in tones of awe; as though such mighty accidents were not for mortal man.

The train was slowing up for Oxford, and the bagman or evangelist or commission agent, or whatever he was, got up, snapped his bag, and was evidently going to get out, when an Angel put a thought into my mind, and I did my Good Deed for the Day. I said, "I really don't know whether you will think I am taking a liberty, but may I buy the book off you?" He said that this did not seem to be fair. I said, "Well, the reason is I shall have nothing to read between this and London, and I am tired of doing geometry in my head." "Doing what?" he said. I said "Nothing; only reading passes the time, and I should really be glad of any book, even that book." He rather hesitatingly accepted my offer; for he was an honest man, and he did not like the idea of my being a shilling out on such fearful rubbish. But he took the coin at last and the property changed hands.

No one else got in at Oxford. The train did not stop before Paddington (it was in the old days before the short cut through the Chilterns). I languidly opened the pages and my heart sank.

The man was quite right (I thought). It was a long time since I had seen those miserable essays, and now, as I turned from one to another, reading a sentence here and a phrase there, I was disgusted. What with affectation in one place and false rhetoric in another and slipshod construction in a third and a ghastly lack of interest in all, I wished from the depths of my soul that I had never made myself responsible for the thing at all. Then my misery was added to by the sudden recollection that it would be my duty, that very week, to gather together yet another sheaf of such chance articles and put them again between covers as I do here and now; for all life is a choice of two evils; and even a bad book to one's name is less dishonouring than a default in payment.

*　　*　　*　　*　　*　　*

Soon the beauty of South England healed this wound and I applied the balm of landscape to my heart until the nasty suburbs had blotted out the view and my journey was done.

Never, from that day to this, have I ever *seen* anyone anywhere reading any of my books. But if I do come on such a person again I shall certainly not examine him upon the effect of his reading.

The Coastguard, or the Balm of the Salt

I HAVE just set down (and you, I hope, have read —since I wrote it for the strengthening of my fellow men) an experience of mine with one of the readers of my books : a man in a train who treated what I had written with great contempt.

Now I have to relate a contrary experience. But I will not say that it happened to myself, for if I did that I should mislead. I will only swear to this, that it did happen to a penman of my own sort, that is, to a man who was not a best seller, and who ground out his livelihood in journalism and little known novels, and who loved the sea. So let *Jonah* be his name.

Well, this is what happened to Jonah; and, in reading it, let the great host of writers lift up their hearts and be comforted; it is, for them, a most encouraging story.

* * * * * *

The Sea that bounds South England has as many moods as any sea in the world, and one of its moods is that of calm vision like St. Monica by the window at prayer.

When the Sea of South England is in this mood, it is very hard upon sailing men; especially if they have

H

no horrible motor on board. For in this mood, there is no wind upon the sea; all lies asleep.

The sea was in such a mood two or three years ago, when this writing fellow, Mr. Jonah, sat in his little boat cursing the saintly calm of the great waters. It was hot; it was about five o'clock in the afternoon; and save for the drift of the tide he had not made as many miles since noon as he had passed hours. Now and then a little cat's paw would just dimple the silky water and then die out again. The big lugsail which was her only canvas (for such breath as there was came aft, and it was no use setting the jib) hung like despair in the souls of evil men grown old. To the North, in the haze, and fairly close by, was England; that famous island. But in the way of a port or shelter, or place to leave the boat till the next free day (and writers never have much spare time for sailing), there was none for many miles.

He had hoped to get into a river mouth of his acquaintance before evening: that hope he must now abandon. It was necessary for him to return to his disgusting labours with the pen, and he was anxious what he should do. With him was a younger companion; and when it was clear that things were hopeless, when the blazing sun had set in a sea of glass, and the long evening had begun, the unfortunate pedlar of prose and verse and rhetoric and tosh saw that there was nothing for it but to take to the oars. Before doing this he looked along the haze of the land through his binoculars and spotted a Coastguard Station. There he thought he would leave the craft for the night. His boat (it was the second and smaller of his fleet) was not too big to be hauled up above high-water mark, and there seemed no prospect of bad weather.

He could return to push her off again in a few days.

They bent to the oars, and before darkness had quite fallen the keel had gently slid up upon fine sand, and these two men, the nib driver and his younger companion, waded ashore with the warping rope, and on the end of it they bent a little kedge to hold her; for the tide had turned and the flood had begun.

They walked up to the Coastguard's house, and were received with due courtesy but without enthusiasm. The Coastguard undertook, however, to look after the boat for an agreed sum, and the column filler, this fellow Jonah, took a piece of paper to write down with his poor fountain pen his name and address, that he might give it to the Coastguardsman.

Then it was that the moment of miracle came!

The Coastguard bent his eyes upon the paper and was transfigured. His whole being was changed. His soul was illumined. His frame shook. When he spoke it was in a voice that seemed to hesitate in his throat with emotion—utterly different from that business-like seaman's tone in which he had hitherto accepted payment for service.

"Can it be" (he said) "that I am addressing the world-famous Mr. Jonah? Not Mr. Jonah the *writer?*—the *great* writer?" The phrase-hawker was very much astonished by this form of address. He had never tasted fame, and least of all did he expect it from such a source, in such a field. He remembered his sixth Aeneid: if good fortune is to come, it will come from a source whence one expects it least of all.

"Not Mr. *Jonah?*" went on the Coastguard, in trembling tones, and reaching out his hand to steady himself upon the table, "The *great* Mr. Jonah? The *writer?* Never did I think that I should live to see this day."

His eyes filled with tears, his voice trembled, and he was silent. But he gazed upon the eyes and nose of the hack with a wrapt, devout air, as upon the features of a God.

Praise is pleasant enough; at any rate, in its beginnings and before a man has had too much of it (for when he is getting plenty of it he will get plenty of hate as well). Fame is always an admirable thing to possess—though publicity is detestable.

The writer, thus finding (towards the close of a long and ill-spent life) Fame trumpeted to him from the lips of a sailor-man, was not displeased. He knew it was his turn to answer and he could think of nothing to say. He murmured the sort of words which he had been taught to murmur to rich women who pretended to have read his books, and who left them lying about uncut on the table when they knew he was to visit their houses. Then a good thought struck him, and he said, "Would you like me to send you one of my books? I should think it a great honour." This was a lie. He did really want to send the man a book, for he was grateful; but it was not true that he felt it to be a great honour. He would have felt it an honour if he had been dealing with a rich woman, but even then he would have worried about the expense.

For I must here digress to tell the reader, in case the reader is not a writer too (and I sincerely hope that she is not)—I must digress (I say) to tell the reader that literary men do not, as the cruel world imagines, get their books for nothing. *They have to buy their own books.* It is a very abominable custom, but so it stands.

He hoped, therefore, that the Coastguard would in his answer leave him the choice of the book, or (better still!) would r ime one of the cheap ones. But what did the Coastguardsman reply? Why, another thing, almost as astonishing as his first speech. He said:

"Oh, sir! I have them all!"

"What!" shouted the inky-one, "*All* my sixty-nine books!"

"Well, sir, all that have anything to do with the Sea."

At this the literary gentleman was struck dumb, for he had not found such faith in Israel.

He said: "May I send you my ——," and here he mentioned a book long dead, damned and done for, but with plenty of the salt water about it; a book written in a very affected manner, and well deserving oblivion.

The Coastguard could hardly believe his ears:

"Oh, sir," he said, "if you will do that it will be the proudest moment of my life! And will you inscribe it for me?"

"I will indeed," said the writer, courteously. So much flattery had turned him for the time being into a sort of Public Person, and he felt himself adopting the tone called, "What can I do for you?": as though he were a politician or a moneylender's tout. So true is it that well-being degrades the soul. "I will indeed," he said. And so he did.

It cost him five shillings, which he could ill afford. He inscribed the book to the Coastguardsman, and posted it.

Ever since then, when Mr. *Jonah* considers the void and waste of a life spent in servitude to Apollo, the tyranny of the God, and his five gifts of Bitterness, Poverty, Contempt, Embarrassment and Drudgery— the gifts he has always given his favourites since he blinded old Homer and sent him about with a dog on a string through Asia, tapping with his stick upon the ground: ever since then, whenever Mr. *Jonah* considers the intolerable waywardness of his Muse (she has not learned the elements of punctuality or of industry in all these forty years); ever since then, whenever he considers the vileness of his writers' trade, and the scorn in which men hold it among the living—he comforts himself with the assurance of some future fame, which must surely be very useful to a man after he is dead.

For he knows—does my friend Jonah—that the Coastguardsman will talk to other Coastguardsmen about his work, and that there will be established at last a sound school of good judges; Coastguardsmen, who will perpetuate his name, whatever the herd may fail to do.

We Are Seven

A MAN of my acquaintance, having heard that William Wordsworth had been described as "God speaking through the mouth of an Englishman," eagerly turned to his published works, of which he had hitherto been shamefully ignorant.

He did not so act through the desire to enjoy the beauties of this great poet, but (I am sorry to say) only with the object of pursuing a foolish occupation of his, little higher than cross-word puzzles or acrostics: one of those manias which men get for games of their own. This practice of his consists in taking famous lines out of the poets, and seeing whether he can improve them by some slight change.

He began doing this under the impression that such a treatment was the test of verse. Someone told him that if verse was of the very first quality you could not improve it by any suggested change.

He was convinced of the truth of this by trying the method upon such lines as the last of the twenty-first book of the *Iliad*, the last of *Paradise Lost*, and the famous phrase in Gray's *Elegy*, "The paths of glory lead but to the grave"; he had long recognised its truth; he could by this method test its poetic value.

He tried "roads," "ways," "tracks," "steps," "march,' "race," "lines," and half a dozen others. But "Paths" stood the test.

So it was then with Wordsworth. He had already played this game of his with hundreds of other poets, when a friend of his, a clergyman, assured him that what was certainly the most characteristic piece of Wordsworth's genius, and perhaps also its highest expression, was a set of four-footed iambic quatrains entitled by the poet himself, "We are Seven": or words to that effect; and that of all this master-piece, the gem was the (repudiated) first line. He did not, therefore, roam at large among the quadrupeds (if I may so call them: I mean the four-footed lines above noted), he took his excerpt at once; only he found it necessary in this particular test to deal with the whole quatrain if he would do it justice.

He used his regular critical apparatus (as he loved to call it); writing down the four lines in large block letters upon a piece of good handmade paper eight inches by five inches, learning them by heart, setting them about fifteen inches from his eyes, then shutting these and attempting his first variations:

> A simple child, dear brother Jim,
> That lightly draws its breath,
> And feels its life in every limb,
> What should it know of death?

The magic of those profound words and of that subtle rhythm possessed him, but did not prevent his courageously making his experiment.

It will interest all my readers, I am sure, to know that, after exhausting every conceivable combination, he registered his conviction that nothing could improve those four lines, and that they were the summit of human expression in their own sphere.

He tells me now, and is willing to tell the world, that the line, "a simple child, dear brother Jim," and the three following it are the chief achievement of our Island Muse.

But he *did* try the experiment of emendation, of a variant reading, before he admitted defeat. He *did* work out a long set of attempted improvements upon that flash of divine genius.

Would that I had room for the whole series, the permutations and combinations of which came to over six hundred examples. I must content myself with a few which are, I think, sufficiently convincing:

> A simple child, dear brother Jack,
> That lightly draws its breath,
> And feels its life all down its back, etc.

Nothing else but "Back" would rhyme with Jack, and evidently the verse was spoiled.

His next effort was:

> A simple child, dear brother Tom,
> That lightly draws its breath,
> And wonders where it got it from, etc.

This last was the only probable or rational third line he could devise, and I doubt whether he could have found a better; yet it is manifestly inferior to the original.

His third effort led to the same result:

> A simple child, dear brother Joe,
> That lightly draws its breath,
> And feels its life in every toe, etc.

His critical sense at once informed him that the particular word "toe" had not the majesty and suggestion of the more general word "limb." There is a sense, of course, in which a toe is a limb, although a very small one, but the effect given by the word "toe" in verse is lamentable. My acquaintance assures me that he has tested the re-action of the word in any number of substitutions, and always found that it lowered the tone of the line, as, indeed, it did in this case.

Thus, "The idol has *toes* of clay," "I sit at your *toes*," "our *toes* are upon the foeman's neck," or, again, "and her *toes* virginal; her virginal white *toes*"; . . . each of these lines seemed stronger when *feet* was used instead of toes.

Since he was compelled by the rules of our Imperial Prosody to a monosyllabic male Christian name, so far as this one termination was concerned, he was driven to "Ned," "Fred" and "Ted," with all of which he could make nothing for the third line, except "and feels its life across its head." Now this was accurate, original, and even arresting; but it gave a suggestion of pain which jarred with the rest of the masterpiece. "Alf" he could do nothing with; and "Bert" was too troublesome to be effectually handled. "James" for "Jim," with "and plays its games" instead of "in every limb," was much the nearest thing he got to what he was seeking.

> A simple child, dear brother James,
> That lightly draws its breath,
> And feels its life and plays its games,
> What should it know of death?

He put it before a great University expert in English literature, who assured him that the spirit at least was worthy of Wordsworth, and that the rhyme was sufficient.

High praise! And yet the effect was not exactly the same, and upon the whole, he thought, inferior. It did, indeed, represent a truth of daily life expressed in daily language, and to allude thus to the games of a little child was worthy and characteristic of the man upon whom another great poet (his successor in the high post of Laureate) has framed the magnificent line, "Him that uttered nothing base." But a gentleman who has lived for many years by writing criticism in the Provincial papers, pointed out to him that the phrase "and plays its games" interrupted the thought after a fashion which so subtle a psychologist as the Chief of the Lake poets would never have permitted.

For my own part, I cannot think that this method of testing the poets is sufficient or conclusive. It may, indeed, be that a line is improved by the substitution of one word for another; but it does not follow that the original line was not itself very great. And we must always remember that we should never have been able to improve it, had not the original suggestion come from the Master Mind.

Thus there is the well-known emendation of Shakespeare's sonnet, "Let me not to the carriage of true minds." The result is certainly better than the original. There can be no "marriage" of minds; whereas the "carriage" of a mind is a common and even necessary metaphor. In the same way Mr. Andrew Lang's suggestion "comes *footling* slow" for "comes *footing* slow" in *Lycidas* is an improvement. So is "The soul of Ananias" (instead of "Adonais") "like a star." So is "no hungry generations turn thee down," and fifty others which genius and progress have suggested in the emendation of originals. But no one of these would have acquired the place they have, had not the original poet given us something to build upon.

Thus, the "Ancient Mariner" may be ended with these lines:

> He prayeth best who loveth best
>   All things both great and small.
> The Streptococcus is the test,
>   I love him least of all.

But are not the original lines—though less vivid and perhaps less noble—the foundation of the later improvement?

I am not sure, as I consider the whole matter, that the best test of any great line of poetry is not that it should be true to Nature, moral (or uplifting) and in perfect scansion. To this rule I would add that if it occurs in a rhymed composition it is essential that the last accented syllable and those which follow it should be exactly similar to the later rhyme on which the ear attends.

On this account I cannot too severely blame the poet William Shakespeare—much as I admire the highest flights of his genius—for making "loved" rhyme with "proved" in the last two lines of the Sonnet above quoted. "Loved" does not rhyme with "proved." Either you have to pronounce "proved" "*pruv'd*," which is very affected, or you have to pronounce "loved" "*looved*," which is really shameful and ridiculous.

On the whole it is safer to stick to blank verse. But that has some subtle scansion of its own which is very perplexing. So perhaps the best medium of all is *Vers Libres.*

124

Talking of Bad Verse

William, you vary greatly in your verse;
Some's none too good, but all the rest is worse.

IT has always astonished me that my colleagues, friends, enemies, and butts, the critics, do not review verse as it ought to be reviewed: I might say, "as *only* it can be reviewed." I am no critic myself; I can say with justice that no living man I ever heard of or met was less capable of criticism than I; but, just as a man who cannot skate may very well judge the antics of people who crash on the ice and go through it, so can I judge the errors of my contemporary critics in the matter of verse.

Surely it is quite clear that there is present, at any moment, either a little very good verse or none.

Poetry is perhaps another matter. I can understand the man who calls poetry so rare that it could only be spotted every half lifetime or so. But good verse, though rare, is not so rare as all that; and, I say again, I marvel that it should not be dealt with as it deserves.

In the first place, there is no necessity for mentioning bad verse at all. Every man and woman who has reached a certain age has written verse. I know of no exception to this rule, save in the case of one woman who has been the occasion of verse in others. Normally, every man or woman writes verse at some time or another. Thirty years ago most of the stuff so written was not published. A certain small proportion was published in the provincial journals of the country, and in the lesser magazines. The tiny remnant that did pretend to be something appeared usually in book form, or, if the author or authoress were in debt, it would first be sold to some important review. Out of this very small number of pieces one could pick the two or three in a year which were good verse. That was the normal way of going on. Occasionally, indeed, good verse was found hidden away among the provincial or magazine stuff and dragged out to light. But as a rule it was hardly worth looking for.

The great mass of bad verse thus turned out— thousands of pieces in a year—went quite unnoticed save by the poetess and her friends. But there arose a little later a new kind of publication imported from America, which is now universal.

In this, verse was used to stop a gap, much as dirty old cloths are used on shipboard to stop a leak, or as any old book will be picked up to make a hoist for the baby's chair at meals. The editor would ask his sub-editor (I have seen him do it): "I want four and a half inches of verse." He was an efficient man and knew what he was talking about. He did not guess the space; he measured it with a little steel rule which he kept for the purpose. Then the sub-editor would answer (also measuring with a little steel rule): "You couldn't space it out, could you? . . . Here's one just over four." This he would answer, referring to a great quantity of verse already put up in type and waiting the moment when it could be so used. Then the editor would say: "All right; tell 'em to lead it."

And so the Muse came to her own.

When this new kind of Americanised magazine had taken firm root in England, the result was a great mass of verse appearing regularly before metropolitan eyes, educated eyes, gentle eyes, traditional eyes, liberalised eyes, trained eyes, generous eyes—upon my soul, I know not what adjective exactly fits; I fear there is not one in the English language, but let us say, "your eyes and mine"; for my eyes are certainly of this kind, and no doubt it will flatter you to hear that yours are.

The next step was the printing of verse in bulk everywhere, and particularly in the high-brow journals peculiar to the literary herd.

At last England was filled with a steady and rising flood of verse, both free and servile; multitudinous; expansive; of a cubic capacity beyond experience.

The tide turned a little before the War; it is still running very strong; it has not yet reached its height.

Nearly all this stuff gets put into books. Even before it gets put into books, notices appear of it in the short reviews dedicated to the periodicals. When it is between covers it receives regular review through a commercial tradition now established in this country that everything which appears between covers must be criticised in print, in order to get advertisement.

With what result? Why, this: that nobody is so infamously bad that she gets some sort of faint praise somewhere, and that the better stuff is lumped in with the worse, and the best with the worst.

I only know of one writer who is consistently ignored, and she is the best of the lot, being in the great Elizabethan line.

I may be told that this way of going on does no great harm, because good verse will pierce at last. I am not so sure. Probably poetry will pierce at last, sooner or later; but on good verse I have my doubts. Poetry is like lightning; you get the flash though the curtains are drawn and the shutters shut; but good verse is only like a strong lamp, and if it is not given its due access it will not be discovered. The reviewers (who are very tired men, having to race round so large a field day after day) have an odd habit of quoting what they think excellent. That gives away, not the reviewers indeed, but the people whom they quote; and as they nearly always quote the quite rotten stuff, one is left none the wiser.

To the jaded mind thus occupied, two qualities seem particularly to appeal; very emphatic rhythm, and subject. When the verse written is patriotic, or sporting, or public-school, or sob-stuff (I say nothing of comic verse, for that is an irritant and left aside) or descriptive of panic or cruelty, or of any other general emotion, one half of the effect is achieved; and if to that there be added the kind of lilt which you get from an engine wheel with a flat in it bumping down an incline, then the other half is added, and the thing is complete. As, for instance:

> Ah, years ago, but I once was there
> And I wish I were there again;
> By Tumty River and Tumty Weir
> Along with the Tumty men.

(I put in Tumpty so as not to offend any school or river, for I would rather die than offend the meanest stream that crawls; but you can fill it in at will, anyhow.)

This is praised; and it ought not to be praised.

By the way, I forgot to add the religious motive, and when I say religious, I mean the vague, the conventional, the pantheistic, and suburban—curse it!

It is responsible for waggon-loads of bad verse; and if it is mixed up with patriotism it becomes intolerable.

The best way out of the trouble is not to review verse at all. Since it must be printed by the haystack and the square mile, why, let it be printed, but let the reviewers leave it free to find its level. As it is, they do nothing but disturb the slow and natural stratification of the muddy waters.

The B.B.G.

MEN are so familiar with the "Blind Beggars' Guild" and its sober but really beautiful uniform in our streets to-day that they take both for granted and hardly ask themselves how the great organisation arose.

I have indeed heard children ask how it was that a lusty, bright-eyed young man striding down the street should be connected with such a name as the " Blind Beggars' Guild" ; but for all of us grown-ups the thing has become a matter of course like the Salvation Army. We never stop to think of the odd incongruity of the name.

Yet the story is fascinating. It is what I have heard Lord Atchamhurst call " a romance of modern organisation," and again, Professor Boodle (now Warden of Burford) has called it in his work on *The Anglo-Saxon Spirit* (Beacon and Co. 17s. 6d.) " a typical, perhaps the most typical, development of an Anglo-Saxon institution from a purely private to a semi-public function."

Before telling the story in the briefest fashion, I must assure my readers that the proof of this article has been submitted to Draga, Lady Pallington, for it would be an offence to the memory of one of our greatest public men if anything should appear of which he would have disapproved; and none could be a better judge of Lord Pallington's fastidious honour than the noble Lady who comforted his declining years.

It was during the depression following upon the first great European war, that the late Lord Pallington (then plain Mr. Powke) found himself compelled, after a very disastrous speculation, to turn to some new field of industry. Having genius, his vision was intense rather than precise: he had no exact plan in his head. He was directed by a trifling accident towards what was to be the success of his life—and a thing of unspeakably greater advantage in his eyes— the foundation of a most beneficent national institution. He was turning over in his pocket some loose change (the jingling of which reminded him ironically that his total available capital was now reduced to £300), when he saw, at the corner of Paradise Gardens in Chelsea, a blind beggar, standing complete with eye-shield, tin mug, little dog and stick, and even the traditional placard hung by a string from his shoulders.

In one moment—how genius leaps where industry must crawl!—a plan arose full formed in his mind.

Mr. Powke first looked very carefully over the standing figure, the dog, the stick, the eye-shield, the tin mug and the placard; then without any hesitation he made his first investment in his new enterprise. He dropped one penny and a halfpenny into the tin mug.

His object in sacrificing the second coin was to call the Blind Beggar's particular attention by the double ring and also to notice whether the dropping of more than one coin appeared to the said B. B. a normal, or an abnormal, event. The thanks he received were purely conventional; that gave him his first hint. It was clear that Blind Beggars were quite accustomed to receive several coins at a time. Their occupation was not unremunerative.

He passed on, turned the corner, so as not to be observed by those who might have noticed his act of charity (let alone by the blind Beggar himself), cast about among the houses facing the blind beggar's pitch until he found one which had a window to let, almost exactly opposite the recipient of his recent bounty. He drew a chair up in front of the window, and watched the Blind Beggar through a pair of strong binoculars, hour after hour.

What command of detail have our modern captains of industry! The future Lord Pallington sat like this without food or drink through all that noon and all the afternoon, noting with a pencil stroke each passer-by and putting a rapid cross against those foolish enough to drop coins into the little tin mug. He was preparing the material for his statistics.

The light dwindled. The April night came on. The blind beggar did not budge, nor did Mr. Powke. He submitted, as must so often the creators of great undertakings in our modern time, to a trial of endurance. It was nearly nine o'clock before a necessity for food shifted the mendicant from his post, and he began to shuffle slowly westward through the now deserted street, tapping with his stick and nervously clutching at the string whereby his little dog led him along.

The moment the quarry moved the hound was

afoot. Long before the B. B. had reached the end of the short street Mr. Powke was walking at a leisurely pace about fifty yards behind him. After perhaps half a mile of this slow progress they came to an open empty space, with railings standing on a broad stone base. The beggar made as though to sit down immediately under a street lamp, and Mr. Powke darted into the refuge of a portico from which he could see without being seen.

He saw the B. B. sit down with a gesture of great relief upon the broad stone shelf, warily lift his eye-shield, glance beneath it furtively to right and left and then, there being no one in sight, remove it, as also the placard; he thrust both into the pocket of his shabby green coat. After that, he turned out from the pocket on the opposite side the coins he had accumulated and began counting them under the electric light above him. Mr. Powke noted that he divided them by shillings, and he carefully counted each shilling that was dropped back again. Now and then a piece of silver would appear and was set aside, when the whole had been put back into the pocket Mr. Powke had accounted for a little over £1 4s. All this done, the B. B. rose and went his way at a brisk pace towards some home of his, still further westward.

Two days were allowed to pass during each of which from morning till night, Mr. Powke sat fixed at his window and marking every passer by and every contributor to the Blind Beggar's cup. Upon the third, Mr. Powke approached the blind beggar and drew him into conversation. He learnt from him the amount of the small levy on condition of which the police allowed him the monopoly of this pitch and one or two other details which, true or false, the man was willing to advance.

The next step was to hire an assistant. For this purpose Mr. Powke laid his hand upon a man with whose past he was familiar, and whose loyalty he could therefore control. He purchased a binocular for him, set him to watch at the window and himself went out to seek other pastures.

He now deliberately chose for his second station a very different quarter of London, near the British Museum, found another Blind Beggar, took up a post of observation (hired for a small tip from the foreman of a stables), and repeated the whole process. He set another watcher there next day, and he did it all over again a third time in Southwark, a fourth in Bethnal Green, a fifth in Hammersmith.

By this time he had accumulated a fairly representative chart of hours, receipts, proportion of donors to passers-by, etc., and he was ready to go forward. He drew up a report upon each of the original five stations, mapped out another five in other parts of the town, planting his watchers as usual and rapidly extending his operations.

Before the end of the year he had one hundred and three Blind Beggars upon his list, of whom twenty-seven were not really blind at all, of whom all but eight were at work before ten in the morning and all but seventeen were on duty till at least eight o'clock at night; only three, he found, made a break in the middle of the day for food, etc., etc. He had a full statistic for his next great advance.

This was to go from one B. B. to the other (acting each time under a different name), and profess friendship and aid, with that sympathy which is so necessary when we approach the poor for their own good.

He began by charitably proposing to each of these one hundred and three men that they should be guaranteed a certain daily receipt, larger that that which they had confessed to obtaining by their own efforts; for he professed to be shocked to hear how little they managed to collect. I very much regret to say that they had all grossly understated their incomes, but those who have undertaken the hard work of uplift will not be surprised at the shocking disregard for truth in that class of society. Meanwhile, he was extending his operations and adding to his tables a second, a third and a fourth hundred, but as his capital was now drawing to an end, he did not extend it beyond a fifth hundred, which indeed covered the greater part of the Metropolis.

Furnished with a complete knowledge, not only of averages, but of detailed receipts, Mr. Powke next undertook the really delicate operation known in higher financial circles as " the Double Cross." He satisfied the police. This done, he played the master stroke and gathered in the whole.

Each B. B. was individually informed that his malfeasance was now known, his true earnings counted, and his false statements upon them exposed. Those who were not really blind were given indisputable proof that their cheat was in the hands of a powerful agent. Each statement of receipt was compared with the real average income. In many cases restitution was demanded and was of course unobtainable. These wicked men who had imagined themselves to be safely fleecing gullible charity sought each his particular policeman—but in vain. The police turned a deaf ear to such appeals, and threatened the B. B.'s with the immediate loss of their pitches if they showed any incompatibility of temper.

After this action, Mr. Powke had all the Blind Beggars of London, real and apparent, in his hand, and was already known among his intimates at the Babylon Bar as " The Blind Beggar King." His original capital had been by this time replenished from his rightful demands upon the miserable beings who had attempted to deceive him, but to whom he deigned to return good for evil. Five hundred Blind Beggars at an average of 10s. each a week gave him an ample income with which to proceed. He provided for articles to appear in the Press denouncing the growth of mendicancy since the war, and urging the necessity for its organisation. He gave the blind beggars pamphlets for distribution, assuring the charitable that accounts were now audited and that a Guild had been formed for protecting their interests, so that no donation.could be wasted upon an unworthy object. As his income grew, he obtained the services of Sir Archibald Glass, R.A., to design a sober but striking uniform with the letters " B. B. G." modestly inscribed in blue upon the lapels of the coat. Lord Lackyer, O.M., the president of the Royal Academy, painted a fine poster, to which the Bishop of Wembley supplied the touching motto " Inasmuch." For the small fee of 50s. Mr. Powke acquired a ringing piece of verse from the noblest and most widely read of our great modern poets, Charles Hagley, which he distributed as an advertisement of his Christ-like efforts. It was set to music by Miss Masham upon a royalty basis and sung as a devotional *Morceau* in many a sacred edifice.

Thus gradually, and by careful, modest, unobtrusive steps, was the great affair built up. Londoners grew familiar with the letters " B. B. G.," the patented symbol of a Red Square, the Poster, the Hymn. They came to know as part of their daily walks in the streets the uniform which guaranteed the control of those who received charity and the proper auditing of donations. Indeed the auditing was conducted by Mr. Powke's own nephew, the name of whose firm stood second to none for integrity. A few abandoned creatures who attempted to imitate the uniform and beg on their own were dealt with severely by the magistrates, who rightly pointed out the special wickedness of such an offence in view of the institution everywhere at work for the public good.

Sir Henry Powke (as he now became in the first Birthday Honours List following upon the second Great War) had long gathered into his magnificent organisation other forms of mendicancy, and, I am glad to say, many of the smaller trades as well, which if they cannot properly be called mendicant, are at least precarious: such as the retail sale of matchboxes, laces, penny toys and flowers, together with boot-

137

blacking and the dissemination of Organs of Opinion owned by the most powerful of our great nobles.

The whole of this superb advance covered less than fifteen years. As is always the case with success, the last efforts of the enterprise were the greatest, and we have remarked within the last twenty-four months the great new Central Offices in Holborn and the District Offices in the various parts of London which have sprung up, with their characteristic Grecian architecture, almost before our eyes.

To-day, apart from the Grand Master, the Wardens, the District Inspectors, the Local Inspectors, Checkers, Accountants and the rest, no less than 7,532 members of the Blind Beggars' Guild now stand upon the rolls, and there has recently been added, standing between the magnificent Enquiry wing of the Central Office and the Employers' Lounge, a department which occupies itself with all the legitimate branches of banking, including, as a special feature, operations in the foreign exchanges.

Lord Pallington did not live long to enjoy the honour which was conferred upon him on the conclusion of his great life work. He died from a very painful form of Cæcopenuria of the Aesthetic Processes, at the comparatively early age of 69 and eleven months. It may be truly said of him more than of any other of his kind in our generation, that if we would seek his monument, we have but to look around. All the old squalor of London beggary has disappeared. Everywhere the bright uniform of the B. B. G. has replaced it and in the whole of that great

138

society (or *family* as the founder preferred to call it) there is not one whose name, antecedents, actions, character, thumb marks, permanent scars, etc., are not in the hands of the public authorities. Best of all, the deaths from starvation have been reduced from 3.337 per cent. to 3.256, and the illegitimate births from 8.932 to 7.615 per thousand. (Decimals to three places.)

The Two Sides of the Sea

WHEN I reached England again the other day after a long journey over much of the West—France, and Switzerland, and Italy, North Africa, Spain, the Balearics, Sicily—I felt once more, at my first landing, the powerful opposition between those closely facing walls of chalk, Kent, and the Artois.

Each time I get back to England from one of these journeys I receive, with increasing strength as the years go on, a certain impression which I have never yet set down in writing, though I have often wished to do so. I will give it now for what it is worth, begging the reader to remember that all such things are personal, more even than most impressions, for they are not corrected by experiences of others. Much of the impression I thus receive must be exaggerated: the proportions cannot be exact; but for what it is worth as a piece of record I will set down the effect which the contrast between Western Europe to-day and South England to-day produces upon me.

In the first place this contrast is a sharp one. It is not to be compared, of course, to the prodigious moral gulf which separates the United States from

Europe; but it is more remarkable than the division made by any other frontier in civilised western Christendom.

You can hardly talk of a frontier between the varied German culture and the French. French and Roman civilisation made the Rhineland, and the influence fades towards the east rather than ceases. Of course, modern conditions, of transport on the material side and of isolated nationalism on the spiritual side, have between them brought Prussian architecture and morals westward. But still, it is a march, not a frontier. There is no cultural frontier between France and Switzerland, nor any between Switzerland and Italy (though it is true you get a sharp differentiation in climate and type between the northern side of any Alpine pass and the southern). Crossing the Spanish frontier (except in the two extremities where the Catalans and the Basques hold both sides of the Pyrenees) is striking; but still, much the sharpest contrast of all is that between any Continental port and its English opposite number. You cross those few miles of water northward or westward into England, and you find a highly separate province of Europe.

The first thing I feel coming in thus to England from abroad is the amazing beauty of its garden. Coming in just at the height of early summer, I felt that more strongly than I have ever felt it before.

Normandy and Touraine have a beauty of something the same kind, but not so arresting. The foreigner who saw it for the first time would be tempted to say that nothing so beautiful could arise

141

in Nature; that it must be the product and design of man. And there would be something in that judgment; for it is the long possession of this earth by English squires, the impression they have made upon their homes, their use of trees especially, which have done most for the result.

I marvel (by the way) that when people debate the pros and cons of an institution they are so slow to quote the strongest case, the truest arguments. There is a great deal to be said against the expropriation of the English people by a small wealthy class, a process which began with the Reformation and was completed during the eighteenth and early nineteenth centuries. There is so much to be said against it that it seems difficult to defend it upon any ground; but if anyone wanted a certain solid fact to bring up in its favour, he might quote the landscape of rural England, the character of that paradise, and especially the conservation of the trees. The old English Peasantry which the Squires destroyed in their greed would never have given us our landscape of park and field and wood.

Next I am struck by the immense superiority of English work in about half a dozen great departments of public activity. The superiority in the handling of ships we all know; but people ought to make more than they do of the English superiority in railway work. There is nothing at all like it anywhere else; nothing in the same class. Certainly not among the Germans, certainly not among the Americans, and notoriously not among the French: the Belgians come nearest, but still far off. For facility of travel, for number of trains, for regularity, and most of all, I think, for physical solidity and smoothness the English railway system is unique. An English express is the only express in the world in which I can write and even repose.

What is true of the English railway system is true of the English Post Office, and, I should add (to the surprise of many), the English Telephone. It is not fair to compare the English telephone system with that of the small countries, for the difficulty of managing a telephone system increases—after a certain point—with the number of subscribers, the area they occupy, and the complexity of inter-communication; nor does it increase in arithmetical progression, but in geometrical. I may be wrong, and men with large commercial experience can correct me if I am; but I certainly know of no other great European country in which this particular department works as well as it does here. You can be absolutely certain, nine times out of ten, of picking up your telephone at any hour of the day or night and getting your communication anywhere, at any distance, within a reasonable delay. In France over short distances, in Germany over somewhat longer ones, I can depend upon securing a room or sending a message, of setting up a plan for which several messages in a short time to many separate points are necessary. But in England it is a matter of course to communicate *anywhere* and at any time, with almost as much facility as one can do it in the Scandinavian countries, where the burden upon the system must be very much less. When I was at Narbonne, for instance, the other day, I should have liked to telephone to Chalons upon a matter I had in hand, but it never occurred to me even to attempt it, so certain was I of interruptions and delay. I would have laid a bet that I should not have been able to get a communication at all, or at least not in what the French call " useful time." But I can ring up, say, Chester from Dover or Canterbury at any time with the secure feeling of getting my communication—on the average—well within the hour, and of getting it clear and good.

The next contrast of importance which I note is that of the daily Press. The English daily paper is better printed and on better paper than the Continental; it is much larger and gives much more space to many more subjects. But it tells you far less about the things an educated man wants to know. Our daily Press is far lower in intellectual standard and news value than the Press of the Western Continent. In France you will get the only papers worth having perhaps a day late, or a day and a half late, if you are in a remote provincial town; but when you get them you read well written, clear, concise, energetic Communist matter in the *Humanité*, or the magnificent writing of Maurras in the *Action Francaise* on the royalist side; or in Italy you may find something by Ferrero in the *Corriere*, and I have no doubt that in Germany it is the same. And apart from the excellence of the writing, you have such real discussion of public affairs, controversy so complete and active, even violent (as controversy should be) that dictatorship alone can prevent its excesses. The

Continental Press gives information on the things that really matter to the citizen. Returning to England, I find murders and divorces, racing and other sports and quite valueless conventional speeches by professional politicians: nothing that really matters, nothing of real moment to the individual or the State. There is a dead silence on the plutocratic forces at work. On foreign relations I find nothing worth reading at all, save now and then an exceptional article grudgingly admitted from the pen of some expert. Even in so actual and vitally important a matter as the Moroccan campaign I found not one intelligent comment, nor have I seen a single map worth looking at. On the day of the Moorish attack north of Taza upon which so much future history turned, the *Times* had a square inch of map with not a point marked on it of all those appearing in its quite obscure telegram, and with the Sebou rising *east* of Taza!

This decline in the social value of the English daily paper has been going on steadily ever since I can remember, and I suppose it will get worse.

Next I notice, on the bad side of English affairs, the lack of organisation for ordinary living; the difficulty of getting proper food; a perpetual offensive interference with the simplest domestic habits such as the rules forbidding a man to get beer or wine except at hours arranged for the convenience and profit of the few great capitalists who control the liquor trade, and who have engineered (to the doubling and the trebling of their fortunes) these increasing restrictions. That one point further illustrates the deficiencies of our Press. I can tell this important truth in a book—I could not print it in any newspaper. And I note in that connection the curious absence of public opinion upon this and pretty well all other matters that really concern our daily lives; hardly any protest against the misuse of the courts of justice or the powers of the police; conventional praise of nearly all official action. I know that this absence of public opinion and this suppression of all essential criticism of rich men's political power are not without advantages; they give the state homogeneity and internal peace; but perhaps these great boons are purchased at too high a price, and we may pay heavily in the near future for our present order through apathy. Moreover, it marks a very great change indeed from the England of only one long lifetime ago, which was far the easiest country to live in from the absence of official interference, and far the most lively in its active public opinion and its vigorous exposure of political disease.

There is another good closely connected with this evil of apathy and lack of public discussion, which good is a universal celerity in official action. Because there is little or no protest against the abuse of public power, public power works like an efficient machine. This is especially noticeable in the processes of law: no nation has more thoroughly reformed or ridded itself of what were—here, also, once upon a time—the delays of the law, and what are still the delays of the law abroad; in no other nation are you so sure of the way in which the closely combined executive and judicial machines will act.

146

Political murder, for instance, has become in France alarming, to modern Italy familiar, and was recently a byword among the Germans. In England it is unknown.

Lastly (and I am afraid this will sound paradoxical, but it is true) there is a certain *level* of excellence in modern English architecture which I do not find elsewhere. I am as much offended as anyone by the abominations of our industrial towns and by the type of new buildings run up to meet the scarcity of houses since the war. But things are worse outside England by far. The new Prussian architecture of the Germans is a stinking offence and the new architecture of France is appalling. I can imagine nothing worse than the new railway station at Rouen or the vile decoration of the Paris Exhibition. Neither would be possible in England. Spain has maintained an admirable standard, but even in Spain you will see things like the new cathedral of Barcelona, which ought to be blown up. The standard in Italy is higher still than it is in Spain, and perhaps Italy rivals England in this excellence of new building. I might put it in this way. That in England and in Italy, but particularly in England, the eye is pleased by one example after another of new work which carries on tradition, which is careful and sound, and which fulfils the eye. It is a very good sign indeed, and what is better it is increasing. On the other hand though there is excellent statuary it is quite sporadic and no general taste is apparent. It is treated, is public sculpture in England, as a sort of mystery in which men must take what they are given, under the assurance that if it is repulsive it must be sublime. Shall I deal with the best things of all peculiar to England, beginning with Bacon and Eggs and Beer? No I began at random and I will end in the same note.

Talking of Fame in Authorship

WHAT is the value of attaching a name to good work? No value at all, I think, save as a spur to action. And I can conceive a condition of Society (in Heaven, for instance) where no such thing need be. But I may be wrong. And I propose to consider later on why I may be wrong.

At any rate, in the first consideration of the thing, there would appear to be no advantage in connecting authorship with achievement. The end of life is happiness. (You have heard that before? You cannot hear it too often!) And the advantage to men in the production of a lovely form in the plastic arts, of final verse, of lucid prose, of complete thought, does not lie in the reputation of the man who may, or who may not, have done the thing. In point of fact, it is not the mere man who does the thing: it is the man inspired. And the reason we are shocked by the vanity of artists is that, more or less consciously, we consider the contrast between what the God has done through them, and their own disgusting selves.

I never knew a man yet who was consonant to his work. Either he was clearly much greater and better than his work, or clearly much less and worse. Now and then you may get a man who is within some

149

appreciable margin of his work; but even then there *is* a margin, and he is above it or below it.

When the work is of genius he is far below it: he is on a different plane. No man is himself a genius. His genius is lent him from outside.

It must be so; because a man's work is but the production of one small part of him, and that small part is driven by powers other than his own as well as by his own powers. Whereas the man himself is the whole of himself. I think we may say of the poet or the artist (and when I say " artist " I mean what my fathers meant and what the poor mean—a person who paints or models; not a writer) that he had better be ashamed of himself as poet (or artist) and concentrate upon the salvation of his soul.

I am moved to these horrible platitudes by reading in an American paper, which has just been sent to me, a number of Limericks. They were ascribed to sundry authors. Every single ascription I knew to be wrong and I said to myself, " What on earth can it matter? " The Limerick is a singular example— and when I say " singular " I mean not odd, but special and unique—of the English genius. There are perhaps 500 of them as perfect in the choice of terms, as exact in cadence, as sharp in surprise, as rotund in fulfilment, as satisfactory in content as anything the Greeks ever did. I am told (to digress) that the Greeks—and when I say the " Greeks " I mean the Greeks, the Greeks of antiquity—were Englishmen, or indistinguishable from Englishmen. I read it in a book only the other day. I did not believe it. But to return. The Limericks produced by the English within the last fifty years are very numerous in their perfection. I have not heard, nor has anyone else, of the certain ascription of authorship to one in fifty of them. Those great poets are unknown. One cannot even say of them as St. Gregory said of St. George: " The Church only knows the names of these; the fullness of their virtue is with Heaven." For we do not know even the names, although their fruits are splendid.

I have heard ascribed to myself in my own presence sharp little verses which I never wrote. And to some of them I have had to say, " Would that I had written them! " though to others I have had to say, " No, thank God, I did not write them." I have also had ascribed to me in my own presence warped and worthless versions of what I had myself written, and once (if you will believe me) I had recited to me a line of my own made better by the reciter's error. There are perhaps a thousand men who have had the same experience in the English language alone, and millions in the long passage of time.

Then there is the case of the admirable thing produced once, and once only, in a human lifetime. The classical case in English is, of course, " a Rose-red city half as old as time." Somebody told me once that the second line ran: "where would you find it, save in Eastern clime? " and that it appeared in a long poem in the heroic metre, throughout the whole of which was not one other single memorable phrase. Then there is the anonymous Highland Boat Song (or Canadian Boat Song); there is the " one crowded hour of glorious life "—and I know not how many other examples of the same thing.

I think one can go further than this. One can say that the great poets live by their occasional successes. The too lengthy writings of all the poets save a very few are like those vast waste reaches of sand in which rocks stand out; the mass of their stuff is ordinary or bad, the hard enduring material is rare and sharply different.

So it comes to this, that the trouble given to finding or announcing authorship is wasted trouble. For the good of man, what matters is the thing produced. For the good of the producer, what matters is his own ultimate happiness in the blessed fields; and there, in Heaven I mean, we may be certain the chance knocking off of a couplet or a statue while we still wallowed on this mud heap of a world will not trouble us very much. Who bothers about the praise of acquaintances when he is in love?

But there is a brief on the other side. Take the converse. Suppose no one were ever allowed to know who wrote this or that, or painted this or that, or modelled this or that. Would not the output diminish? It would. It even might, for what is an odd reason, cease. The reason (it seems to me) is this: that the very best work, especially in verse, takes root in very early manhood; its seed is sown in childhood. Now in very early manhood we are ambitious. Fame seems to us at that moment a good in itself. Lacking that spur to action we should not act. The roots would not strike. The tree would not be confirmed. Once the thing is done and the habit of production running

152

strong, then, as we all know by experience, work, good or bad, will be done to the end of the chapter. So it is all in the providence of God, and this itch for ascribed authorship has its place with every other itch. Blessed be itch.

I have written "work will be done to the end of the chapter." Therein I am certainly right. The habit of production established, it will continue. But am I equally right in suggesting that ambition, the desire for fame, dies with age? Upon second thoughts I am not so sure.

I know a man in English letters now nearer sixty than fifty who gets as hysterical over an unfavourable review as a boy of nineteen. I have heard that Victor Hugo was much the same. And I well remember an aged member of Parliament coming to me once in the Lobby at Westminster and crying in tones straight from the heart, "Oh, I say, Harmsworth has only given me half an inch!" I also remember a man who got into a railway accident (through no fault of his own) in the late 'sixties, and who, when I was a young man in the late 'nineties, still talked of nothing else than that accident. For him it was a sort of authorship. It gave him glory. He was, within his own mind, the maker of all the railway accidents of the world: the chief actor of Ferro-carrilian smashes: the Archetype of Express-gebrashting.

But really, when it comes to glory, there is no limit to the absurdity of man. A man will glory in a disease, a vice, the wealth of an ancestor when he is himself poor, or the poverty of an ancestor when he is himself rich; the street in which he lives; the colour of his hair, of his eyes; the possession of something which he picked up in the street—even abuse from someone more notorious than himself. Man will glory in anything, just as the famine-struck will eat anything. Such is the appetite for glory. And why is it there? I say again, to make men achieve: to make them write bad verse, build hideous houses, put up impossible monuments, pass bad laws, and in general destroy their kind.

The Fate of a Word

I WONDER what will happen to the word "gentleman"? What has happened to the thing we all know. What will happen to the idea of the English gentleman, or rather to its memory, is more important, but does not for the moment concern me. What I am musing upon is the fate of the word.

The whole language is going through a very rapid change. It is liquefying. The change is not one of form, it is one of use; not unlike the changes that happened to Latin after the beginning of the great transition towards the end of the Pagan time. In that language you can take the word *comes* and see it changing its application while it keeps its form. Indeed, we have the form still, and from having meant a pal with Scipio and a Crown's delegate with Augustus, it means to-day a count (or an earl), having meant in between a Judge, a high Civil Servant of the Empire, a General, the Administrator of a County, and lots of other things. And there was the word "schola," which begins (I believe) by meaning leisure in Greek, and to-day means a place where people are taught, or a set of studies; having meant (in between) almost any conceivable form of association, from a club to a company of infantry, and having meant also a hostel, and a hundred other things. You could make out a list of any number of Latin and Greco-Latin words which behaved like this when the great transformation of the antique world began.

Well, what is going to happen to the word "gentleman"?

To-day it is in the most dreadful state. It is used variously by various classes, societies and nations. It is used variously *within* each particular society or class. It is used variously by the same individual.

It has, so far as I can make out, only one precise meaning (but then few of our common words to-day have precision, so it is not wonderful that this word should have only one precise use). When it is used thus, it means "a male possessed of the habits which are instinctive to that which once was the English governing class." It means exactly that, and nothing else, when it is used in the only sense where a sharp form distinguishes it. There is the gentleman's accent, the gentleman's way of eating and drinking, and the gentleman's everything else. It has nothing to do with being a good man or a bad man, nor even, strictly speaking, with being a rich man or a poor man; though, of course, the habits could only have arisen in a leisured and therefore wealthy class. That is the meaning of the word in such a question as, "Did he speak like a gentleman?" which the mistress of a house will ask of a domestic who opens the door to some unknown person. The connotation is that the domestic, being familiar with the gentry, will catch the accent as the surest hall-mark.

Then there is the meaning at the other end of the

156

scale—the vaguest meaning of all—where the word "gentleman" attaches to the idea of any male whose name is unknown and to whom reference has to be made cautiously.

Some years ago this use was a class use. The gentry themselves had no such practice. Half a lifetime ago it was even a matter of jest on the part of the wealthier classes that such a euphemism should be used by people poorer than themselves. Gentlemen laughed at non-gentlemen who would ask concerning another non-gentleman, "Who is that gentleman?" To-day, it is pretty well universal; though there are patches of society which it has not invaded, as for instance, seafarers. If a man helps to pull up my boat above the surf in Chesil Cove, I do not say, pointing to a bronzed lad with earrings, "We must get that other gentleman to help us." It would be out of place and sound ridiculous. But I should use the word in a shed where the boat was being overhauled; I should say to the carpenter, speaking of his mate, "Could that gentleman lend me a two-foot rule?" I should use the word here because the man to whom I was speaking would expect it. In that particular place, a boat builder's yard, the word would not be universally used; but it certainly would be universally used in any good shop in town. One would say, "No, it was another gentleman who accused me of stealing the tie-pin."

Then there is the whole series of meanings in which it has a more or less emphasised moral content, signifying the presence of some good. The very same man will say of an old man enriched but of obscure birth, "He is such a thoroughly good man that it is a pity he should feel awkward because he is not a gentleman"; and, of the same old person, in another connection, will say, "I never met a man who was more of a gentleman." In the first case he is using the word in its precise meaning; in the second in a totally different one, attaching to qualities of the soul and especially to a sort of courteous charity.

If the English language had remained the idiom of one highly differentiated country, homogeneous and possessed of a classical tradition in speech, all this would not have happened. The English language was still in that state when Carlyle wrote (nearly a century ago) that he was disturbed by finding no gentleman's face among the Frenchmen in a Channel steamer; or, if not disturbed, at any rate moved to contempt. Carlyle, of course, knew nothing of the world. He might as well have expected kangaroos in Scotland as English gentlemen in a French crowd. But his use of the word shows that it had a precise meaning in his mind. To this day you hear people sometimes remarking that they hardly ever see what they call a gentleman abroad except in Germany or Scandinavia; and you know exactly what they mean. They unwittingly express a religious sympathy.

But the flux cannot go on for ever. The liquefying process will stop, and crystallisation will succeed it. Now what form will the crystallisation take?

I think it likely enough that it will take the form of entirely separate uses, like those which have come to attach to a rider of horses. To act in a "cavalier" manner is an utterly different thing from acting like a "cavalier" at Naseby. You do not necessarily expect chivalry from cavalry, and when a gangsman in Spain roars out *"Caballeros !"* at a group of workmen whom he wants to recall, he has no idea of horses or of horse-riding in his mind. It would not be surprising to read in a criminal charge a couple of hundred years hence, "the aforesaid gentleman"; or to find that the infantry of an armed force had come to be called "the gentlemen."

When the differentiation has fully taken place, we shall have in this particular, as we now have in countless other cases, a confusion of history. The historian of the Victorian period, before Fustel had transformed historical science, gaily mangled the Latin terms of the Dark Ages, because he read into them their classical meanings. He knew, indeed, that some of them had changed, but he was quite wrong upon the greater number: as, for instance, in the case of that word "school." When the Saxon King went off to make his soul at Rome he was said in our histories to die "in the school at Rome," but it was not a school at all in our sense; it was an inn founded for English pilgrims.

I fancy that the same thing will happen to the man reading documents of our time some centuries hence. The literary form which will guide him will probably be that of the eighteenth century, for it was then that English most nearly reached a classical standard and was least loose. The word "gentleman" will connote, for the scholar, membership of a certain class based upon the ownership of large estates in land: what we still call "Squires" and the Germans "Junkers."

Having that idea in mind, what a hash he will make of our documents! What contradictions he will find! How desperately he will be puzzled! Just as we are puzzled by the word *"miles"* in the accounts of Hastings; so that reading of 50,000 *"milites"* under the command of the Conqueror, the number seems impossible and has even led fools to deny the evidence of eye-witnesses. And later we have the same trouble with "Servi."

Which leads me to this last consideration. Of a thousand adult males in England to-day, how many are gentlemen in the precise sense of that term? One at the most, and how many in the widest sense of that term? Certainly over nine hundred. Now what will posterity make of that?

True Advertising

IT is now some months since great numbers of men concerned with advertising came from all over the world (except Europe, Asia and Africa) to belaud, to worship and defend their religion of advertising. They reminded one of a Church Council in the fourth and fifth centuries.

The conclusion of their debates, the dogma established after these Fathers had thrashed it out, was that advertisements ought to tell the truth.

Lord, how my heart leapt up to find that after so many disappointments, after seeing defeated so many causes which I have loved, so many gallant men gone down into the darkness and so much wickedness triumphant, this one piece of good had appeared in the miserable chaos of our time! Advertisement, I told myself, as I went home meditating the glad news, is in future to be True! Advertisements are no longer to lie!

They will continue, no doubt, to offend everyone of our senses (except that of smell) with every form of vulgarity. They will still present to us the successful City Man with his aquiline nose, white moustache and considerable Adam's apple in a lean throat. We shall still have children called "kiddies." We shall still have our procession of beautiful young women playing

L   161 with beautiful children, while a not beautiful, but at any rate, happy and quite young father, comes home with a mass of chemical foods. We shall still have dresses hung on to women so flat that they recall the Yale type of key and with faces flatter still. We shall still have horrible old scoundrels with a Houndsditch leer appearing as old family butlers, English squires, Scotch lairds of the early nineteenth century, French cooks, or anything else which the artist has to illustrate. We shall still have (I sincerely hope) what I like much better because they give me a pleasure free from all contempt of my kind—I mean those pictures where people are represented as suffering from the conse- quences of not using the thing advertised. I have before me as I write (to quote the ready-made phrase of the politician making for a lie) several examples of this which I have cut out from this morning's paper; for they gave me so much delight as I came along on the top of the 'bus that I did not mind the rain. In one of them there was a most miserable object drawn about in a bath-chair, and close by him a woman fainting and upon the point of death, all because they did not eat some stuff or other, the name of which I have forgotten. Then there was a perfectly glorious picture of a man dashing away the inkpot with his left hand and upsetting it, his face in a crimson frenzy, his hair bestormed—and all because he cannot get at his telephone. There is another of a person whom I recognise most familiarly: he is sitting with his head between his hands, his elbows on the table, his face haggard, and before him an indescribable litter of unsorted papers of every shape and size and certainly more than 3,000 in number. You can almost hear his groans. Yet if he had used a contraption of drawers and files, which for hideousness beats the Epstein Memorial by four lengths, he would not be like this at all. He would be fat and jolly and smiling and crammed with self-satisfaction and as ready for hell as any man can be in this imperfect world.

I say we shall have all these types going on, but the advertisements will be *true*.

How different our newspapers will become and our walls and the works of our great artists! Then, indeed, will what is called "advertising matter" be worth reading. Then, indeed—in this new time which the advertisers have decreed—shall I linger lovingly over the great monstrosities upon the hoardings. Then indeed shall I say to myself, "I forgive them their crudity for the sake of their enormous entertainment."

Thus we shall have a man writing:

"Buy my chocolate—it has not got enough sugar in it and chocolate without enough sugar in it is disgusting. The chances are that the chocolates you will buy will have been made some weeks, and stale chocolate is a horror. Also, if you saw it being made you would never eat it again; nevertheless, buy my chocolate because I only have one million pounds and I want to get two million together before I die."

That would be a true advertisement; and I who had thought that I should never live to see such things, am now about to have them shovelled at me by the score. How true it is that some lives, after long struggle, end in blessedness!

I suppose the people who sell chemical food in any of its hundred forms will write something like this:

"This stuff which I am putting up in tins for you may be easily described. It is made from the flesh of the pig: honestly it is. Not from any part of the pig in particular, but just from any or all parts chopped up. Most of the pigs were healthy, and your chance of getting part of a bad one is quite small. On the other hand, it is only fair to tell you that I have put in a poison to keep the stuff from putrefying, and I have put in another chemical, not poisonous, to give it colour, and another chemical, which is only poisonous in very large amounts, to give it consistency. That is all I have to say about it. *P.S.*—Even the poisonous chemical is not there in such large quantities as to do you any immediate harm. Your health will gradually suffer, but you won't feel any acute physical pain until you have got a great accumulation of it into your system after many years."

Then we should have the brewers: "This beer is not made with malt. It is made of a stuff called glucose, treated with sulphuric acid and other jolly things. There are no hops in this beer. The bitter taste is got by the use of a certain drug, the name of which for the moment I forget; but I have written to my chemist at the brewery, and in my next series of advertisements I will tell you what it is. This beer of mine does not satisfy your thirst, for I have put a certain amount of salt into it in order to make you want to drink more."

Then we should have the motor car manufacturer: "The only difference between my car and the others is

that I am the manufacturer of it. Anyone can manu-
facture a motor car: or, to speak more accurately,
anyone with capital can exploit other skilled men,
poorer than himself, who know how to work in metal,
and get them to make a motor car. The difference of
value between motor cars is simply the difference in
the excellence of the work and the power of the motor
car. Have you got that? If you buy my motor car,
I shall become rich. If you buy the other man's, I
shan't. That is all there is to it. *P.S.*—The price at
which I sell my motor car is just over twice what it
costs to make. The difference goes in bribes, advertising, commissions, blackmail and interest to the bank."

Then we shall have the "Society for Doing Good":
"Do not forget to give your pence or your pounds to
the 'Society for Doing Good' (the S.D.G.: you will
know it by the little blue zig-zag: that is its sign). It
has a slogan: which is a damned vulgar outlandish
word, meaning a phrase to hypnotise with. Its slogan
is 'All for God.' It supports twelve hundred clerks,
touts, managers, bullies, spies, and others, of whom
I, at the head of the advertising staff, am one. I have
a little villa at Cheam, which I have not yet paid for;
so do please contribute to the ' Society for Doing
Good.'"

Then we shall have the New Moneylender's
circular. I look forward to that!

"I was born in a Galician ghetto. They call me
Mrcwz. I have come to the only land where such as I
are sacrosanct, and where no one will dare speak of
my origins or challenge my new name of Howard. I
have set up as a moneylender because I hear that it

leads to the highest honours in your State. I charge sixty per cent., but you pay mightily more than that before I've sucked your blood out of you. I shall take all you have and get a clutch on all your life and bring you down to dishonour and death: but before you die you shall see me among your peers with the title of some dear English town of yours. Believe me, I loathe you well."

Any one would reply to a circular like that. Those in use to-day are poor stuff and catch not one victim in a hundred with their stale lies.

Then there arises before me a last little advertisement which I have always so longed to see and have never yet seen, and which ought to run something like this: "Really good things are rare. Men do not get to know about them, and in this evil world they are under a curse. I do not for one moment believe that you will buy my fountain pen. You will go on using the other fountain pens which leak great blobs of ink, which run dry, which get cross-nibbed, and which also have an abominable way of getting lost just after you have bought them. My fountain pen runs smoothly and sweetly, carries ink for a month, never gets clogged; and when you think you have lost it, it comes back to you wagging its tail."

The reason I say I am waiting to see this advertisement is that I did, many years ago, have a fountain pen of exactly that sort. I have never been able to find one since, and I have forgotten its name. But if that advertisement comes out—and I suppose it will when the True Advertisement Stunt is well-launched —I shall recover the treasure and be at peace.

On Talking and Not Talking to People in Trains

IN the matter of talking (and not talking) to people in trains there would seem to be two branches, according to whether one wants to talk in trains and be talked to, or whether one doesn't.

So that the subject naturally divides itself into two sciences, or arts, which may be collectively called "silentiorum ut gabbalorum cultus"—the art of making people talk to you although they don't want to—and the art of making them stop talking to you when they do.

But these are mere titles and headings. The art is an art, and an art is a woundy difficult thing. However, I will give such rules as I have myself acquired by experience and a few of those communicated to me by others: and this I will do out of my love for my fellow-men.

We will begin with the simplest side, which is the art of stopping people who want to talk to one in trains. The amateur's way, which for my part I greatly despise, is to answer briefly, growl, frown, continue reading, begin writing jerkily upon the margin of the paper, and so on. You have all done it. It is ill-bred, uncharitable, leaves a bad atmosphere in the carriage and, what is worse, is often unsuccessful. If three or four want to talk, it is useless. There are other ways.

The first and best (but it needs what parsons call "character") is to reply by contradictions.

The enemy says "It looks as if it were going to rain." You answer as offensively as you can, "Not it!" The meekest man will bridle up and say, "Oh, you don't think so, don't you?" Then you answer, "No, I don't!" and the chances are he dries up. But if he is word-hungry, pursue him. If he goes on, for instance, "Well, I've always found it rain with that kind of sky," answer, "You have, have you?" If that doesn't stop him and he still continues with some such remark as "Yes, I have!" combatively, you can break off the action by saying, "Well, I don't care to go on discussing it, anyhow," and you are free.

If you feel that you have not the "character," as it is called, for such abominable conduct (but remember that great fortunes have been made through indifference to human suffering), there is another way, which I will now disclose to you. It is called the Self-Depreciatory—and it is infallible.

I take the same gambit. The enemy opens, "It is going to rain." You answer, sighing, "Yes, worse luck!" He (surprised): "Why 'worse luck'?" You (bitterly): "Because when it rains, I run amok!" At this, seeing the way in which fermented liquor is being given a sort of nasty religious position in our miserable time, he will probably glance at you with a horrible suspicion and fall back on silence, whereat

168

you can turn again to the *Police Gazette* or the *Times Literary Supplement*, the *Empire Review* or the *Christian Science Monitor*, or whatever it was you had wickedly invested in to feed your hatred of mankind.

Supposing he doesn't stop but goes on to ask you whether you cannot control the craving, tell him no, you can't, because it is hereditary. You know very well that it is leading you to destruction, but it is too strong for you altogether. If he then tries to convert you by arguments drawn from instances of his own experience, affect the utmost misery and assure him that in your case it is far, far too late. If he still persists, make a real scene, wring your hands, shout and make life intolerable to him. I have never known an instance in which it was necessary to go so far. It is nearly always efficacious to begin with one startling confession, though you may, if you like, clinch the effect when he is in retreat by continuing little confidences; he is pretty sure to take an attitude and show that he wants to know no more.

Another way, more dangerous, but exceedingly useful, is to feign madness. You need not go so far as that peer who, now not long since, would, when any-one spoke to him in a train, pull out a large Norwegian knife and begin to strop it lustily upon the window strap. It is enough to answer intriguingly.

The enemy says " It is going to rain." You put on a cunning idiot look, you lisp and say, " Ah, that's right ! " with which you smack your lips and roll your eyes. It should frighten him off. If the first check is not enough and he tries to go on ner- vously by asking whether you mind rain, lean forward

169

to him with a meaning look, wink and say, " No, I *like* it!—and there's a reason! "

I have no room to go into the four other classic methods of stopping conversation in trains, for I have now to deal with the sister art of luring into conversation those who are determined not to talk at all.

The first and sovereign method is not of my own experience but was told me by another.

It seems you can nearly always get the poor blighter to break silence, however determined he may be not to talk, if you have a companion; and the method is to say to this companion (if you have no companion, any honest-faced stranger will do), " I am glad they have put Wembley on the site of the old Crystal Palace." Your companion, if she is a confederate, must answer that she did not know where Wembley was but that she is glad to hear it. (If you are handling a stranger, not a confederate, he will deny your statement.) Then must you begin to curse and to swear and to say that you are absolutely positive, and that you were at Wembley only yesterday and part of the remains of Paxton's horrible old conservatory were still standing. It is impossible for a Trappist to stand up against such an attack. The most silent man will burst out against your monstrous lie. Then it is for you to play him. Allow yourself to be gradually convinced; but do not gaff him into your basket until he is tired out. Get a run for your money.

Another way, not quite so good, is to stretch out of the window, clutch the door, stare forward and shout, " Oh, my God ! " It does not work unless you put your head right out of the window. The

170

dupe will think there is going to be an accident and will ask you in alarm what is the matter. You must then affect relief and say, " The danger is past! " making up I know not what lie, but having thoroughly shaken him up out of his shell. The chances are that he will go on talking, and you must lure him to this by a detailed description of some interesting accident of which you will say that you were a witness, although you were not. He will then tell you that his uncle was in a railway accident. This also will be a lie. But you will go on to ask him whether he remembers accidents in the past, and the fire will be well alight and burning merrily.

Another way (so contemptibly easy that I hardly recommend it) is to feign sudden illness. People in trains, unlike the rest of the human race, have very kind hearts. You need not shriek; a few groans are enough, and who knows but that the fellow may have a flask upon him? When you are better, you will find yourself fast friends in full conversation.

Yet another method, savouring somewhat of the first, but in a chapter by itself, is to sit down comfortably after the train has started for a long non-stop journey (as to Bath) and say, " Well, that's all right. A fair run to Swindon ! " There is no living man— no, not even though he were dumb—who will not be moved to speech by this trick. On hearing that the train will not stop at Swindon you must make a convulsive gesture to catch the little chain which runs through the carriage and costs £5. The enemy will certainly seize your wrist if you are slow enough. Allow yourself to be persuaded. Tell him in great detail the dreadful consequences that follow your failing to meet your aunt at Swindon. You will have a long and pleasant conversation all the way to Bath. You will be the more certain of this happy issue if you make the story turn somewhere upon money. For appetite, avarice and fear are the three motives of the human race. Appetite is often lulled to sleep, fear you may not be able to excite, but to avarice you can always appeal by bringing in some talk of money.

And this mention of money leads me to my last method, or at any rate the last which I have strength to set down. You can always provoke conversation in trains by the prospect of gains whether it shines or whether it rains. If the stubborn man will not yield to a hint of gain in stocks, try horses. If he will not yield to horses, tell him about a reward (offered by the railway company) for anyone who will spot cracked walls along the line. If that fails, talk of some way of doing the journey cheaper. Anyhow bring in money somehow and you will milk conversation as by a sort of physical necessity in the Holy Spirit of Man, which is always charged with an over-burdening consideration of money and money and more money.

I must add one more. Ask your opponent for a match. When he has given it to you, let it go out and ask for another; then ask for a third. There will be objection, apology, and you will be a witless man if you cannot hook such origins on to a really interesting discussion upon the fate of the soul, the future of Great Britain, cancer, or whatever else may take your fancy.

On Rasselas

THE other day I saw, I held in my hands, a first edition of *Rasselas*. I bowed down and adored.

I had known the book in every form all the days of my life, for those from whom I come have worshipped it before me and have possessed it I suppose, in one edition and another, all those years since first it came from the press. They must have had the first edition in their time, but it has not come down to me.

I do not agree with those who pretend that first editions are a vanity. Great wealth will divert them from their proper function and place, as it will divert anything in these days. It will add something precious, ridiculous, and vain to the idea of first editions as it will add folly and pretence and false luxury to such admirable things as the sailing of a boat and hunting.

But the first edition of a great book is a thing to be revered. It carries with it (I know not why) something of immediate contact with the author, and of the air in which it was written. Anyone who has been brought up on the first edition of a great work will never feel the same when he reads it in another form. As a child I read *The Rose and the Ring* in the first edition, which our family had had from Thackeray, and I cannot feel the same of any other. I learned my Dasent's *Tales of the Norse* in a first edition, and all others seem to me degraded. I read my *Masterman Ready* in a first edition, and when I gave it to my own children I was at pains to get hold of a similar copy. I could not bear that they should feast upon that admirable story without the proper furniture of the good square English type, the solid rag paper, and the charming woodcuts, which all went together in my mind with the tale told, and without which the old sailor was not himself.

But to go back to *Rasselas*—every man ought to read *Rasselas*, and every wise man will read it half-a-dozen times in his life. Indeed, a man would do well to read it once a year at least; for never was wisdom better put, or more enduringly; and if it be true that the test of a book is the mood in which we lay it down, then this book must have as high marks as anything ever written in English and, therefore, the highest marks of anything ever written in the world.

It came out a few days before *Candide*, and men customarily contrast the one against the other; giving, of course, by far the higher place to Voltaire. But here, in my judgment, they err; for I will stoutly maintain the commonplace that a work of art is not to be judged wholly nor even generally by its effect as a work of art, but is rather to be judged by its whole social effect upon man. If it be a piece of writing and that writing fiction, and that fiction fabular, then one great part of our praise must attach to the attraction of the fiction, the fable, the style. But these

174

are not all. There is also the prime question whether the book be noble or ignoble, moral or immoral, whether it does us good or harm; and our most general judgment must depend upon the old test imposed upon us by the ancients, the mood in which we lay it down.

Now a man laying down *Candide* is in a mood of delight in its wit and of satisfaction with its style—polished jade. He may even obtain some moral advantage from the ridicule of much that is worthy of ridicule. But upon the whole, he will have found good things to be so much hated by the author and the best things to be so poisonously attacked, that either his mood will have something of bitterness and disgust, or, if he takes satisfaction in this attack on decency and good, it will be because his mind was already tainted before he took up the volume. No good man is the better for having read *Candide*, but every man is the better for having read *Rasselas*.

I will even confess (but this I know to be personal and not generally defensible) that I am much better fed by the style of Johnson than by the style of Voltaire. The second is like the blows of a hammer chiselling out a marble statue of great perfection, but the first is like the rhythmical swell of deep water; and I prefer that movement; it suits me better. Moreover, while Voltaire is lapidary and will pack a sentence tight with meaning leaving it still quite clear, Johnson nearly always, and especially in *Rasselas*, puts all there is to say of a considered judgment—and a true one—into the antithetical form, than which no better medium has ever been discovered for condensing and preserving a conclusion. Voltaire's economy is like a sphere: the maximum content for its surface. Johnson's is like strong soup: a concentration of nourishment:

> "Some are the slaves of servants whom they have trusted with their affairs. Some are kept in continual anxiety by the caprice of rich relations, whom they cannot please and dare not offend. Some husbands are imperious, and some wives perverse; and, as it is always more easy to do evil than good, though the wisdom or virtue of one can very rarely make many happy, the folly or vice of one may often make many miserable."
>
> "If such be the general effect of marriages," said the prince, "I shall, for the future, think it dangerous to connect my interest with that of another, lest I should be unhappy by my partner's fault."
>
> "I have met," said the princess, "with many who live single for that reason; but I never found that their prudence ought to raise envy. They dream away their time without friendship, without fondness, and are driven to rid themselves of the day for which they have no use, by childish amusements, or vicious delights. They act as beings under the constant sense of some known inferiority, that fills their minds with rancour, and their tongues with censure. They are peevish at home, and malevolent abroad; and, as the outlaws of human nature, make it their business and their pleasure to disturb that society which debars them from its privileges. To live without feeling or exciting sympathy, to be fortunate without adding to the felicity of others, or afflicted without tasting the balm of pity, is a state more gloomy than solitude; it is not retreat, but exclusion from mankind. Marriage has many pains, but celibacy has no pleasures."

I would maintain upon this long extract (and I could pick you out a dozen as good in the short work) that it has these four qualities—What it says is (1) true, (2) important, (3) of good moral effect, and (4) packed.

There are some men who think that concision is a

176

matter of short sentences and short words. It is not so. Concision is a matter of giving what you have to give in the least compass compatible with lucidity; and Johnson pulls it off.

There are whole stacks of novels giving one criticism and another of marriage; half of them strained in epigram, and not one of them clamping down the truth in its frame as it is done here in *Rasselas*.

I am glad to say that Johnson was well paid for *Rasselas*. And I am also glad to say that he took very little trouble over it. I am a humble colleague of that great man, being myself a hack writer, and I know how much any of my brothers in slavery is to be congratulated upon good payment for an easy job.

He promised to write it in five days; he did write it in under seven. He used only a few of the later hours of each day at the task, and he was paid what would correspond to about £400 to-day; that is, he was paid a sum which would keep a man in a very quiet middle-class way for a year. He was paid one hundred pounds; and one hundred pounds in the middle of the eighteenth century would do that, just as four hundred pounds will barely do it to-day. He had even better luck, for though he sold his copyright (which is always a mistake—but I do not know how the laws stood in that time; they are still offensively unjust to the sons of Apollo) his bookseller voluntarily gave him, I believe, another £25 when he saw the thing selling. That has never happened to me. I sold a book once out and out for a tiny sum in my youth. It has gone through thirteen editions and I have seen none of that further money it has earned. But, after all, if you sell a thing you sell it, and you have no right to complain.

So much for *Rasselas;* or rather, so little. It is a book round about which a man might write for ever; solid stuff; beef; good roast beef with Yorkshire pudding; real roast beef, not your modern baked stuff, but beef roasted from a jack in front of a great coal fire.

*   *   *   *   *

After so writing of *Rasselas*, my American friend Colonel Isham (who has perhaps the best collection of Dr. Johnson's work, and of everything around it) showed me another copy of that great book and one to be treasured, in my judgment, more even than that first edition which moved me so greatly.

It is Mrs. Piozzi's own copy—the one she had in old age; and upon page after page it is annotated in her own clear and beautiful writing, more than a hundred years ago.

Now here is an amazing thing! Here is something in which all the elements of historical value arise—the living contemporary witness, the intimate witness, the original document: all combined.

It is nearly certain that this woman, upon whom the great Englishman's affection centred so strongly during all those last years when he was increasingly lonely with the hubbub of fame about him, was born in 1740. She was thirty years younger than he, she outlived him by half a lifetime, for she did not die till she was eighty-one years of age. She died the same year as Napoleon.

178

It is curious to note that this copy, in which she has made so many annotations, is as late as the year 1818. It is Sharpe's Edition. That writing of hers, therefore, which we here see so small and so clear in the margin of page after page, was set down in the very last moments of her life, when she had approached, or had passed her eightieth year, and when the book itself had been in the hands of all Europe, and famous, for just on sixty years.

Here was this vivacious, energetic, admired old lady, living on into a world over which the storm of the French Revolution had passed and steeping herself in the memories of a youth more than half a century dead. She had been a girl of nineteen, perhaps barely that, when *Rasselas* first issued from the press. She returned to it in the very extreme of life when death was before her, who had lived life so fully, and when she could write as younger people cannot write.

In the margin on the corner of page 8 she has written:

> Man feels from home in this Life but rests and expatiates in the World to come.

She writes thus, in age, as an annotation to Johnson's phrase:

> Man surely has some latent sense for which this place affords no gratification, or he has some desires distinct from sense, which must be satisfied before he can be happy.

The book is of small size, about eight inches by five inches, and has perhaps a dozen of those very careful little steel engravings which are so characteristic of the day.

It is a lady's book altogether, and it is a lady's mind commentating perpetually on as manly a piece of work as was ever set down by a man. Also sometimes (but rarely) she dares to underline at the risk of defacing the page; and, herein again, she was a lady of her day.

I find underlined four words upon page 99 at the end of chapter 27, at the end of the Princess Nekayah's discourse upon " Whether perfect happiness would be procured by perfect goodness "—that admirable speech which begins, " Whether perfect happiness would be procured by perfect goodness this world will never afford an opportunity of deciding " (I wish I could write like that!) and again, " All that virtue can afford is quietness of conscience, a steady prospect of a happier state : this may enable us to endure calamity with patience: but remember that patience must suppose pain."

Johnson's vivacious, active young friend, now grown so old, underlines in this last phrase the words " enable," " endure," " patience " and " suppose."

I would argue with the Doctor (if he were alive and before me now, and promised not to roar too loud) upon that matter of a quiet conscience. I do not believe that good men have quiet consciences. I hold that an uneasy conscience—at any rate nowadays—is the first requisite for Heaven, and that an inflamed, red, feverish, angry conscience is a true mark of increasing virtue. I have met many men with quiet consciences, not all of them wholly unintelligent, but nearly all of them scoundrels.

Mrs. Piozzi (for I must not leave the lady alone any

longer) has further added, " Some diseases are caused by virtue as some are by vice." Yes, Madam! And many more by virtue than by vice! I know of no disease striking down a swindler or one of those rich beasts who are for ever thinking of their body's health, or the vile fellow who would rather drink water than wine: I do not say who is ordered water by a doctor, him I can forgive, but who drinks it of his own accord and glories in it.

The oppression of the poor brings no disease to a man. But generosity embarrasses his finances and brings him to loss of sleep and sometimes to madness. Indignant virtue has even worse effects. Patriotism, if it be too active, will land him in the tortures of a gaol; and of nervous indigestion there is no more common cause than deep affection withdrawn or gone awry.

But to go back to Mrs. Piozzi and her *Rasselas*.

There is not in all this monument of Johnson a truer or a more profound phrase than that which I find annotated a little earlier in the same chapter:—

" Discontent," answered Rasselas, " will not always be without reason under the most just and vigilant administration of public affairs."

Which is as much as to say that complaint against government is a permanent and essential necessity, even where that government is exceptionally good. It is an imperative duty in common times; in times of plutocratic corruption, such as our own, it is a crying and immediate necessity if the State is not to die of the poison.

Mrs. Piozzi writes by the side of this: " Well

observed and to me new; except having once read it in Italy." She quotes the name of an Italian author or subject, which I cannot decipher, and then a translation of his words, " Men in Power are no Gods."

How excellent also is the following. She finds Johnson saying through the mouth of the Princess, " He does nothing who endeavours to do more than is allowed to humanity." Mrs. Piozzi puts by the side, " True, true, make your Decision and be content," and then, " Quod sis, esse velis."

I could write all day upon this singular treasure of a book. Let me find room for two last citations. The first is from words written fairly early, I think, in the course of this marginal work of hers, for they were written while her hand was still quite steady.

On the last page, page 184, below the final line of the text and the words " The end," followed by a full stop, Mrs. Piozzi has cut out the full stop with a dash, and has added in her own handwriting " of a Book unrivalled in Excellency of Intention, in Elegance of Diction: in minute knowledge of human life—and sublime Expression of Oriental Imagery."

But the most touching, the most arresting sentence, is what may have been, I think was, the last of all her pen work on the paper of this volume; for it is written in a larger and trembling hand, surely a little before she died. It is in connection with the passage in chapter XXXVI upon the progress of sorrow. Here again the Princess is speaking and says, " What is to be expected from our pursuit of happiness, when we find the state of life to be such that happiness itself is the cause of misery?" and to this the old woman's shaking fingers add, "*Oh melancholy Truth, to which my heart bears witness.*" And after that comes only a long quavering line.

A Chinese "Litany of Odd Numbers"

THE NINE NINES, or NOVENAS

The Nine Deplorable Social Habits.

> Drunkenness.
> Dirt.
> Shuffling.
> The Loud Voice.
> Scratching.
> Unpunctuality.
> Peevishness.
> Spitting.
> Repeated Jests.

The Nine Admirable Social Habits.

> Relieving of Tension.
> Courteous attention.
> Discreet mention.
> Tenacious retention.
> Assiduous recension.
> Wise abstention.
> Calculated prevention.
> Tactful intervention.
> A sense of dimension.

184

The Nine Follies.

To think oneself immortal.

To think Investments Secure.

To take convention for Friendship.

To expect a reward for right doing.

To imagine that the rich regard you as an equal.

To continue to drink after you have begun saying to yourself that you are still sober.

To write verse.

To lend (or still worse, to give) money.

To travel with much luggage.

The Nine Rules for dealing with the Poor.

To be courteous.

To be distant.

To oppress.

To exploit.

To pay little.

To pay exactly.

To pity vaguely.

To interfere.

To denounce to the Authorities.

The Nine Rules for dealing with the Rich.

To flatter.

To attend.

To remember many faces.

To love none.

To hate very few.

To attack only the defeated.
To enrich others by counsel.
To enrich oneself by all means whatsoever.
To lie.

The Nine Negative Rules for Walking in the Country.

Not to fear beasts.
Not to walk without an object.
Not to become self-conscious when another
    approaches.
Not to hasten or linger but to adopt a dull
    stride.
Not to avoid trespass.
Not to avoid mud.
Not to avoid hills.
Not to brood on trouble.
Not to walk when you can ride, drive or
    be carried.

The Nine Negative Rules for Walking in Town.

Not to talk to oneself.
Not to barge into others.
Not to swing the cane.
Not to cross the street in a reverie.
Not to neglect a salute.
Not to contest authority.
Not to purchase unnecessary wares.
Not to despise the evil eye of beggars.
Not to leave a fallen coin lying.

The Nine Jollities.
    To laugh.
    To fight.
    To fulfil the body.
    To forget.
    To sing.
    To take vengeance.
    To discuss.
    To boast.
    To repose.

The Nine Final Things.
    Disappointed expectation.
    Irretrievable loss.
    Inevitable fatigue.
    Unanswered prayer.
    Unrequited service.
    Ineradicable doubt.
    Perpetual dereliction.
    Death.
    Judgment.
        [Here end the *Nines*.]

    THE SEVEN SEVENS, OR SEPTETS.

The Seven Hateful Things.
    Scorn from a woman loved.
    Acute pain of the body.
    The memory of shame.
    Insult accepted from the rich.
    Defeat of one's country.
    Seasickness.
    Despair.

The Seven Rare Things.
    Vision.
    Recovery of things past.
    Good cooking.
    Being loved.
    Satisfaction.
    Remarkable wine.
    Justice.
The Seven Common Things.
    The mother's love.
    Embarrassment.
    Quarrel.
    Ambition.
    Disappointment.
    Misunderstanding.
    Appetite.
The Seven Delightful Things.
    Deep sleep.
    Conscious vigour.
    Reunion.
    The Landfall.
    Unexpected praise from a loved woman.
    Resurrection.
    Final beatitude.
The Seven Medicines of the Soul.
    Remorse.
    Repentance.
    Submission to the Divine Will.
    A wide landscape.
    A sublime air of music.
    A firm determination to combat evil within.
    Believing by an act of the will.

The Seven Medicines of the Body.
> Work.
> Bed.
> Combat.
> Riding.
> Bread.
> Wine.
> Sleep.

The Seven Stenches.
> The Traitor.
> The Pervert.
> The Cruel Man.
> The Sly Man.
> The False Teacher.
> The Deserter.
> The Politician.
>> [Here end the *Sevens*.]

THE THREE THREES OR TRIADS.

The Three Oddities.
> The Dwarf.
> The Giant.
> The Foreigner.

The Three Standbys.
> A Loyal Friend.
> A Good Wife.
> A Stiff Boat.

The Three Perils.
> The World.
> The Flesh.
> The Devil.
>> [Here end the *Threes*.]

THE TWO TWOS, OR PAIRS.

The Two Things Worth Having.

Virtue.
Mutual affection.

The Two Things to be Rejected.

Pride.
Sloth.

[Here end the *Twos*.]

The One Thing of Both Good and Evil Effect.

Honour preserved.

[Here ends the *One*.]

Talking of Poverty

I HAD occasion the other day to give an address to a number of young men upon the matter of Poverty : which address I had intended to call " Poverty: The Attainment of It: the Retention of It when Attained." But I found that no title was required, for Poverty was familiar to them all.

In giving this short address I discovered, as one always does in the course of speaking without notes, all manner of new aspects of the thing.

The simple, straightforward view of poverty we all know: how it is beneficial to the soul, what a training it is, how acceptable to the Higher Powers, and so on. We also know how all those men whom we are taught to admire began with poverty, and we all have, I hope, at the back of our minds a conception of poverty as a sort of foundation for virtue and right living.

But these ideas are general and vague. I was led by my discourse to consider the thing in detail, and to think out by reminiscence and reason certain small, solid, particular advantages in poverty, and also a sort of theory of maintenance in poverty: rules for remaining poor.

I thus discovered first of all a definition of poverty, which is this :

" Poverty is that state in which a man is perpetually anxious for the future of himself and his dependents, unable to pursue life upon a standard to which he was brought up, tempted both to subservience and to a sour revolt, and tending inexorably towards despair."

Such was the definition of poverty to which I arrived, and, once arrived at, the good effects flowing from such a condition are very plain.

The first great good attendant upon poverty is that it makes men generous. You will notice that while some few of the rich are avaricious or mean, and while all of them have to be, from the very nature of their position, careful, the poor and embarrassed man will easily share whatever little he has. It is true, that this generosity of the poor man flows from no good motive, but merely from a conviction that, whatever he does, it will be much the same in the end; so that his kindness to his fellows is a mixture of weakness and indifference. Still, it breeds a habit; and that is why men whose whole characters have been formed under this kind of poverty always throw away their money when by any chance they get a lump of it.

Then there is this other good attending poverty, that it cures one of illusions.

The most irritating thing in the company of the rich (and especially of rich women) is the very morass of illusion in which they live. Indeed, it cannot be all illusion, there must be a good deal of conscious falsehood about it. But at any rate, it is an abyss of unreality, communion with which at last becomes intolerable. Now the poor man is physically prevented from falling into such vices of

192

the heart and intelligence. He cannot possibly think that the police are heroes, the judges super-human beings, the motives of men in general other than vile. He can nourish no fantasies upon the kind old family servant or the captain of industry, his supreme intelligence. The poor man is up against it, as the phrase goes. He is up against the bullying and corruption of the police, the inhuman stupidity of the captain of industry, the sly, self-advancement of the lawyer, the abominable hypocri-sies of the old family servant. He comes across all these things by contact: by direct personal sensible experience. He can no more think of mankind as a garden than a soldier can think of war as a picture, or a sailor of the sea as a pleasure-place.

We may also thank poverty (those of us who are enjoying her favours) for cutting quite out of our lives certain extraordinary necessities which haunt our richer brethren.

I know a rich man who is under compulsion to change his clothes twice a day, to travel at set periods to set places and to see in rotation each of at least sixty people. He has less freedom than a schoolboy in school, or a corporal in a regiment; indeed, he has no real leisure at all, because so many things are thus necessary to him. But your poor man cannot even conceive what these necessities may be. If you were to tell him that he had to go and soak himself in the vulgarity of the Riviera for so many weeks, he would not understand the word " had " at all. He would say that perhaps there were some people who liked that kind of thing, but that anyone should do it

N

without really liking it he could not understand.

And here's another boon granted us only by grinding, anxious, sordid poverty: action.

There is no greater enemy of the Soul than sloth; but in this state of ceaseless dull exasperation, like a kind of grumbling toothache, sloth is impossible.

Yet another enemy of the Soul is pride, and even the sour poor man cannot really nourish pride; he may wish to nourish it; he may hope in future to nourish it; but he cannot immediately nourish it.

Or, again, the Soul is hurt by luxury. Now poverty in the long run, forbids or restricts luxury.

I know very well that you will tell me with countless instances how the poor gentlemen of your acquaintance drink cocktails, eat caviare, go to the theatre (and that in the stalls), take taxis, order liqueurs with their coffee and blew cheques. Very true, but if you will narrowly watch the careers of such, you will find that there is a progressive decline of these habits of theirs; the taxis get rarer and rarer after forty-five, caviare dies out, and though liqueur with coffee goes on, the coffee is on that account less frequent. There is a real discipline, incredible as it may seem, imposed upon luxury by poverty. Indeed, I met a man only last April in a town called Lillebonne (where I was examining the effects of Roman remains upon hotel-keeping), and this man told me that before the War he habitually spent his holiday (he was a parson) in Switzerland, but now he could not get beyond Normandy. Whereupon I sketched for him on a piece of paper a scheme showing, with a radius vector (the same graduated, which, indeed, was my parson, also) and drawn to scale, the expenses of a holiday. Therein did I show him how a holiday killing lions in East Africa cost so much, another badgering the French in Morocco so much, another annoying the Spaniards so much: and how the cheapest holiday of all was a holiday on foot in Normandy which lies but one poor Bradbury from the coasts of these islands. This little diagram he folded and took away —little knowing that a still cheaper holiday could be taken in the Ardennes.

Poverty has a yet nobler effect by its introduction into our lives of irony: and irony I take to be the salt in the feast of intelligence. I have, indeed, known rich men to possess irony, but only by importation, just as a man may possess a picture which he has bought. Poor men possess irony as native to themselves, so that it is like a picture which a man paints for his own pleasure and puts up on his own walls. All the poor of London have irony, and, indeed, poor men all over the world have irony; even poor gentlemen, after the age of fifty, discover veins of irony and are the better for them, as a man is better for salt in his cooking. Remark that irony kills stupid satire, and that to have an agent within one that kills stupid satire is to possess an antiseptic against the suppurative reactions of the soul.

Poverty, again, makes men appreciate reality. You may tell me that this is of no advantage. It is of no direct advantage; but I am sure it is of advantage in the long run. For if you ignore reality you will come sooner or later against it like a ship against a rock in a fog, and you will suffer as the ship will suffer.

If you say to the rich man that some public fellow or other has genius, he may admit it in a lazy but sincere fashion. A poor man knows better; he may admit it with his lips, but he is not so foolish as to accept it in his heart. In the same way a rich man growing old will try to forget Death: but a poor man, especially if he has children, keeps Death steadily before him.

And indeed the very best one can say of poverty is that it prepares one very carefully for the grave. I heard it said once by a beggar in a passion that the rich took nothing with them down to death. In the literal acceptation of the text he was wrong, for the rich take down with them to death flattery, folly, illusion, pride and a good many other lesser garments which have grown into their skins, and the tearing off of which at the great stripping must hurt a good deal. But I know what this mendicant meant—he meant that they take nothing with them down to the grave in the way of motor-cars, hot water, clean change of clothes and various intolerably boring games. The rich go down to death stripped of external things not grown into their skins; the poor go down to death stripped of everything. Therefore in Charon's boat they get forward, and are first upon the further shore.

And this, I suppose, is some sort of advantage.

On "Dating"

THE French have an expression which has been partially adopted in modern English literary work, though it has not, I think, come to stay, for it is foreign and exotic. They talk of a literary work's "dating." They would say of the *Yellow Book* or of Tennyson's *Idylls of the King* that " they date." And the meaning of the phrase is, of course, that the thing criticised seems to have sunk, from its first position in general esteem, and to have so sunk through the effect of an old-fashioned savour emerging and overweighting the intrinsic merit of the work.

The term expresses a certain quite clear truth in literary and artistic affairs, a truth which we all recognise. Stuff above a certain level is major to the fashion of its time and masters it; stuff below that level is minor to the fashion of its time and is mastered by it. Stuff above a certain level is like a beautiful woman whose portrait we see well painted; no matter what the fashion of clothes in her day, the excellence of the painting, the beauty of the human being dominate any preoccupation we may have with the accessories. On the other hand, if the portrait is of a sort of beauty merely fashionable at the moment and not permanent, or if it is of flashy, ephemeral, superficial workmanship, then the accessories dominate the main subject and we say that " it dates." So the phrase " dating," or " it dates," conveys a blame: a relegation of the thing mentioned to the plane of disfavour. I have given two examples. To take one of them—*The Idylls of the King*—everyone, I think, will be agreed upon the distinction between what dates in these and what does not. For while there are passages in them which are too great for this sort of blame, the bulk of them are clearly subject to it.

The truth is that this phrase " it dates " indicates but one section (the first in order of time) of the process through which excellence, especially in letters, is decided by the test of survival.

It is a most mysterious process. I have never seen it sufficiently analysed, and I am certainly incapable of analysing it myself. There would seem to be various strata of critical judgment in the mind, of which the topmost, or superficial, is the least to be considered, and of which the lowest and least conscious is the most permanent. Or, perhaps, the truth is that an inferior thing, greatly admired in its own age, suffers under the test of time because that contemporary mob which admired it and made its short-lived reputation, had no rooted feelings, nor any permanent, instinctive canon of criticism. Thus its enthusiasms are easily forgotten, and the task of final judgment is handed over to those who feel strongly and permanently.

At any rate, time does sift the gold, especially in letters; and this process of " dating " is the first step in the descent of that which was overrated.

198

But there is something more in the phrase " it dates " than the mere consideration of time. Of two things not first-rate, one will sink of its own weight, without suffering this degradation of dating at all, and the other is perceived to be inferior precisely because it has about it so strong an aroma of perished fashion. For instance, the greater part of Wordsworth's work does not date: it is remarkably bad, and there is an end of it. It might have been written pretty well any time in the nineteenth century. But the mass of Bulwer Lytton's work, which is quite as bad, dates fiercely.

Now what is the distinction between the bad stuff that dates and the bad stuff that does not? I take it that the distinction lies in the presence or absence of hypocrisies, of affectations.

A man sits down to write a sonnet—I say " sits down," but it may take many years to write a sonnet. No matter, that is the conventional phrase. He sits down, I say, to write a sonnet. He cannot write a good sonnet. He can only write a bad sonnet. He may do one of two things. He may, like an honest cow, set down the bad sonnet just as it occurs to him; ending up for instance, with the couplet:

"Oh, England! Oh, my country! What a place
Of habitation for the Saxon Race."

If he act thus, he sinks quietly into oblivion without shock or offence, and if he is overrated in his time, no memory of the false reputation remains to disturb his eternal sleep. But if, conscious of his incapacity, he tries to dope himself and his reader with tricks of poignancy peculiar to his time, then he will inevitably "date." The essential intimate act is one of humbug.

The man knows that he is not inspired, but artificially instructed, and he can only use the dodges of his time. For instance, all Oscar Wilde dates, except one or two profound horrors in *The Ballad of Reading Gaol*. Vernet, in painting, dates damnably; though he only meant to paint badly, yet he could not avoid certain sham effects of his time (and here I may add that all our modern trick painting—that is, pretty well all our modern painting—will date nauseatingly before many of us reading and writing to-day are dead).

There is a first-rate example of the evil which makes dating (and the corresponding virtue which avoids it) in the work of Greuze. Greuze had two styles: one of sugar, or rather of glucose, and the other of sound wheat and wine. You would say in comparing, for instance, any one of his pictures in the Wallace Collection with such a striking thing as the Robespierre—which was and is, I believe, still in the possession of Lord Rosebery—that they were painted by two different men. But they were not. The difference between them is that Greuze had to do the best he could to make a living (with a nagging wife), and found certain sentimental tricks of his time producing money. All that he did thus hypocritically and (since he was an honest man) unwillingly dates like a crinoline. But what he did sincerely and as he chose to do it does not date at all.

I think one might almost say that the writers who have the supreme gift of sincerity may be thus tested. I mean that those of them like Swift, who do not date at all, are thereby proven to be, what Swift to his glory was, sincere through and through.

But I would add two *caveats* modifying such a judgment. The first is this: if a man has to write or to model or to build or to paint (like poor Greuze) too much at too rapid a rate with too sploshy an output, if he is compelled to do it by poverty or some other form of constraint, then he will date, however sincere he may be. He will date in places and not in others. Even Gilbert dates here and there. Next, it must be admitted that there are some artists of their nature so excellent that they are apparently incapable of bad work, or at any rate of letting it be seen by the world. These cannot date, but the merit does not lie in their sincerity; it lies in their incapacity to be insincere. For there are some artists who, unless they are doing very well, are doing so badly that they shock themselves with the result, and will suffer poverty or any other evil rather than produce it before the world.

Let me add that of all " dating," the worst, the most laughable, the most obviously condemnatory, is not artistic " dating " at all, but the " dating " of physical science.

The way in which the physicists have bawled out revealed and unspoken truth at the top of their voices during the last seventy years, each absolute dogma promptly contradicted by some new doctrine immediately succeeding it, dates these worthies as are dated no practitioners of any other trade. And they are very closely followed by the people called the Higher Critics, for in both there is the same fundamental intellectual absurdity, the essence of which is taking hypothesis for fact, and firmly believing things without authority and without sufficient proof.

Talking of Epitaphs

SOME time ago I read a notable article on Latin epitaphs. I was moved when it came out to write a letter to the paper, telling of one or two others I had come across, which seemed to me beautiful; but I feared I might intrude upon what was already a very complete collection. However, I have stored up quite a number in sundry languages (I only know three with smatterings of a fourth); all are, I am afraid, commonplace; but for what they are worth, here goes.

The first two I have already registered in a book of travels. I found the one in Tunis, the other in Algiers. The first was

Ecclesia mater :
Theophilus in pace.

It was, I am told, a tomb of the early third century, or even of the late second.

The next was of a Pagan priestess on the rock of Constantine:

Ingemuerunt Dryades.

But indeed, all that land is full of memorials to the dead. And further west, in Morocco, I read of, but did not see, an epitaph which ran (I do not know the original language):

When I asked who lay here, they told me "two lovers," and I
made the gesture of compassion.

202

Then there is the famous legendary tombstone of Brittany:

> He by him and she by her.

Everybody knows " *Miserrimus !* " and all that are worth calling " all " know very well what is not an epitaph, but a mystery scratched upon the scaling stones of Balliol:

> *Verbum non amplius Fisher.*

What is perhaps less well known is that excellent quatrain which I came across in a chance newspaper the other day, and which I pass on inaccurately to my fellow-men (it is indeed a case of saying " pass on "):

> Reader, pass on, nor waste your worthless time
> On lying eulogies and far worse rhyme.
> For what I am this mound of earth ensures;
> And what I was is no affair of yours.

I have always discovered a powerful irony in the simple epitaph:

> Here lies M. N., an unknown, who was found perisht of starvation in this Parish on the 25th December of the year of our Lord God 1737. *Resurgam.*

There is also one which I cannot accurately set down, but which runs something like this:

> She was a kind and excellent mother, an industrious house-wife, a devoted spouse; none the less, all who met her were fatigued by her disagreeable humour, and she was unable to obtain (in this life) the praise she surely deserved.

I say that I have not got this verbally accurate, but they say that reading epitaphs destroys the memory.

Gibbon writes justly of the motto (and tombstone) of the Courtenays:

> What I spent I had, what I gave I have, what I saved I lost—

that they must have lost a good deal; seeing that when

they affixed this epitaph they were the richest family in Europe.

Mark Twain registered a fine one which he found in his journeyings, " The light was restored to her " on such and such a day of such and such a year. It was of a blind woman. And he found another which he has also recorded, of a husband and a wife, beginning: " Here lies so and so, in such and such a year, awaiting her mate," and then in a different character, fifty years later, " Who has come." To which one may add the Hottentot proverb:

Patience is a well in the depth of which lies heaven.

A friend told me of a roughly painted epitaph upon a wooden board in the graveyard of some German soldiers in France:

Here lies so and so (a private soldier) He died fighting bravely and is buried far from his dear Fatherland.

Now, detestable as is the use of the word " fatherland " in the English language (which has the much finer word, " country ") it is difficult not to translate this German into a barbaric term of the same original sound.

It is clear that epitaphs should be lapidary; not because they must be graven upon a stone (they may be run in bronze, which is more enduring), but because death has a complete unity about it and requires a stop-short for its expression. Therefore the very long epitaphs upon which the rich spent so much money in the eighteenth century, are thrown away.

Nevertheless I have always thought those epitaphs where a single name is inscribed to be bombastic.

They savour of that vulgar pride which makes titled men of lineage mumble their names when they have to give their address, instead of pronouncing them clearly. Those who put a single name on tombstones take it for granted that everybody will know what is meant by the name, and will worship the great shade below. It is asking too much. If we came to-day across a stone on which was deeply chiselled " William Shakespeare," and if it stood above his tomb, we (or, at any rate, all of us who are sane in the matter of the controversy) would be moved; but the single word " Chateaubriand " seems an exaggeration. He wrote admirably; but he will not, any more than Byron, take full marks. Put him in the high seventies or low eighties. Such an epitaph is usually cut just after a man dies, and that is too early for moderns to be certain of his place.

Nobler, I think, are those epitaphs which give the name and the principal functions: nothing more:

> He enlisted as a private soldier in the year II of Liberty, was promoted to lieutenant at the end of Ventôse, captain in Messidor, of the year III, Major in Fructidor, Colonel of his regiment in the same year, and General Officer in Nivose: appointed Commander of the Army of the ——— in Frimaire of the year IV. He died of fever on the 10th Pluviose, having conquered in fifteen actions and two campaigns and having captured 17,532 prisoners and 8 guns.

That seems to me to fill the measure. As the American lady said to the foreign prince: " Prince, it's a mouthful."

And talking of epitaphs, what could be better than Gautier's :

> Ci-git Clarimonde
> Qui fut de son vivant
> La plus belle du monde.

205

But in the way of epitaphs (although it is not an epitaph, but an epigram—anyhow they both begin with " epi ") surely the greatest of all, the hackneyed, the immortal, is the Heliodora: which, for the love I bear it, I will now write down; what is more, although I know no more of Greek than the Sphacterian goat, I will dare translate:

> You are down there under the earth, Heliodora; and I shed tears for you at this end of our love in death. They are bitter tears; but what I so present upon your tomb, so mourned, are the memorials of such a love and also of such a friendship! I, Meleager, cry aloud for what I loved, even there down among the wasted things. But there—I only pour out an empty gift to Acheron. God! Where is that Beloved, my Beloved? The darkness has snatched her away. The darkness has snatched her away and dust is defiling the flower in the height of its bloom. Do you then, Earth, I pray to you, who nourish us all, take Heliodora, whom all so mourn. You are the mother of us both. Take her gently in your arms, to your breast.

Δάκρυά σοι καὶ νέρθεν ὑπο χθονός Ἡλιοδώρα
  δωροῦμαι, στοργᾶς λείψανον, εἰς ἀΐδαν.
δάκρυα δυσδάκρυτα· πολυκλαύτῳ δ' ἐπὶ τύμβῳ
  σπένδω μνᾶμα πόθων, μνᾶμα φιλοφροσύνας.
οἰκτρὰ γὰρ, οἰκτρὰ φίλαν σε καὶ ἐν φθιμένοις Μελέαγρος
  αἰάζω, κενεὰν εἰς Ἀχέροντα χάριν.
αἰαῖ ποῦ τὸ ποθεινὸν ἐμοὶ θάλος; ἅρπασεν ἀΐδας,
  ἅρπασεν· ἀκμαῖον δ' ἄνθος ἔφυρε κόνις.
ἀλλά σε γουνοῦμαι, Γᾶ παντρόφε, τὰν πανόδυρτον
  ἠρέμα σοῖς κόλποις "μᾶτερ ἐναγκάλισαι.

It is Pagan; that great foundation from which the Greater Thing arose; and I tell you without boasting that I, who have no Greek, can never read this thing without an inclination to tears.

In my ignorance I leapt to the conclusion that some pestilent critic or other had tampered with this gold and had turned ὑπὸ into διὰ because, not understanding the power of repetition, he thought that διὰ made the stuff less repetitive. But I wrote to the man who knows most about these things in Britain. Now he told me that both those readings existed. That the first was from the Palatine manuscript, but that the latter was from the Middle Ages, and that the Palatine had greater authority. He said, however, that most editors think νέρθε δια is wrong, but conceals something else, such as νέρθεν άεὶ.

Of these things I know nothing. But I am quite certain that a man who says " down there underneath the earth " is writing like a poet, while the man who says " down there through the earth " is writing like a beastly modernist.

Talking of epigrams which are also epitaphs, there is that other one in the anthology, of which I will not trouble you with the Greek, first because I do not know it by heart, and therefore cannot write it down here, and, secondly, because you have had quite enough Greek for one meal. But Professor Phillimore has translated it thus:

> Once did we sail the deep Aegean swell,
> Who in this midland plain of Asia lie.
> Glorious Eretria, once our home, farewell!
> Athens, Euboea's neighbour land, goodbye.
> *And now goodbye to thee,*
> *Thou well-beloved Sea.*

A threnody is not an epitaph. But it is of the same world, and therefore I may say here in passing that Dean Inge in his Latin elegiacs upon his daughter has written the greatest Latin thing of our time. He has touched the mark of the Ancients.

Verse on the dead is not an epitaph, but it is of the nature of an epitaph, so let me quote:

> Roland my friend, young gentleman and brave
> (*Amis Rollanz, prozdum juvente bele*),

which is out of the Song of Roland, and that other line which may be called the epitaph of Turpin, the Archbishop:

> Turpin lay dead in service of the King.
> (*Morz est Turpins el servise Carlun*).

I have quoted it so often that I have a right to quote it again, like that Canon of Chester who ceaselessly repeated the story of the Pied Bull, an excellent Inn. Well, then, to conclude—is that epitaph, I wonder, well known upon one Ilarion? It is Macaronic: in part Latin and in part English.

> *Laude tu Ilarion audacem et splendidum*,
> Who was always beginning things and never ended 'em.

I think not.